NOURISH:

Exploring the Intersection of Food

and Human Connection

NOURISH:

EXPLORING THE INTERSECTION OF FOOD AND HUMAN CONNECTION

BY AMENDA LEE

NEW DEGREE PRESS

NOURISH
Exploring the Intersection of Food and Human Connection

ISBN	978-1-63676-713-0 *Paperback*
	978-1-63730-054-1 *Kindle Ebook*
	978-1-63730-156-2 *Ebook*

Table of Contents

This book is dedicated to my grandma and grandpa, dad, mom, sister, and best friends, Anaïs and Tiffany.

"Food can be expressive and therefore food can be art."

– GRANT ACHATZ

Introduction

———

The Beginning

Ever since I was a child, I was intrigued by the *act* of cooking. I remember begging my mom to help in the kitchen, whether that was by preparing huge jars of spicy kimchi, chopping colorful vegetables for savory soups, or sampling bites of side dishes to test for seasoning. The often-chaotic atmosphere of the kitchen excited me, and in the sounds of the venting fans, bubbling pots, screaming hot pans, and ticking rice pots, I found solace. I remember the playdates I spent with my friends at my house, insisting they try my food creations, which were often something simple, like a slice of toast with cheese melted on it. For me, it was less the flavor of the food I was interested in—it was all about creating something greater than the sum of its parts that could be shared with others.

The Present

At my current age of twenty years old, the same approach to cooking fuels my passion for it. Although I may be working out of a different kitchen, experimenting with different cuisines, one thing remains constant—the revolving door of friends and family at dinnertime.

The mentality of food as a gift translates to my motivations for cooking now, as I prepare to enter my last year of undergraduate education at the University of Southern California. Some of my fondest memories during my college years include the home-cooked or family-style meals I shared with my friends. Other food-related experiences during this time were not so positive, like my battle with multiple eating disorders and body dysmorphia. However, overcoming the disordered eating habits typic of these years has allowed me to rediscover my passion for delicious meals while being mindful about my mental and physical health. Ultimately, food and cooking have construed the basis for fostering and maintaining positive relationships with my friends and myself for almost the entirety of my life.

Many people may only see what food is at its most basic—a necessary element to life, something that gives us energy and fuel. While this interpretation is factually sound, it shows an incomplete definition of what food really is to *humans*. For us, food not only nourishes the physical body, but it also nourishes the soul. Whether that is through personal friendships and relationships or a reimagined version of the self, food can be a vehicle of creative expression, love, happiness, multiculturalism, faith, and empowerment, all while being the connective tissue that binds us together. It can be political or it can be simple. Regardless of what it can represent, humanity's relationship with food is complex and unlike that of any other species.

As a naturally introspective person, I wished to further explore the different connotations of what food represents to humanity. But just like humanity, food is diverse and multifaceted. In writing this book, I hope to relate my observations about human interactions with and around food to my reflections of the world and how I fit into it. For humans, food is so much more than an energy source. It is art, it is communication, it is love, it is culture. At the same time, it can be capitalized on, shared, purchased, or made. My musings on food are meant to start an internal conversation, one that helps others consider the meaning of their own existence through the lens of food.

My current kitchen and where I engage in creation

Speaking of my lived-in experiences, I can't speak about food without explaining my own complicated relationship with food. One reason why I emphasize the multifaceted aspect of food is because throughout my life, I have been through the emotional wringer with food. Sometimes, I absolutely loved the art behind cooking and romanticized food. At other points, I struggled with loving food—in fact, sometimes I hated it. During other periods, I even overcomplicated my relationship with food while diminishing it to solely its identifying numbers, like calories. Therefore, I will speak about my history with disordered eating throughout the book in relevant sections. I would advise someone who is easily triggered by eating disorder discussions to be aware of these topics before they occur, so they are able to decide whether or not to read this book or certain chapters for themselves.

A constant state of restriction led me to assume this position many times in front of an open refrigerator.

This book is for people who love food *and* for those who have lost that connection with cooking or food. In fact, if food exists as simply an unremarkable, necessary part of your routine, this book will probably change your outlook on how you fuel yourself.

- I will discuss stigmas about eating disorders, even one that has not been recognized by the *Diagnostic and Statistical Manual of Mental Disorders* as an eating disorder or mental illness, meaning less insight is shed on the topic.

  - As someone who has struggled with many different disordered eating behaviors, such as orthorexia, a condition where one becomes obsessed with the nutritional makeup and caloric value of different foods, I explicate how recovery can be just as difficult as illness itself. I also share the tools I have personally used to improve my relationship with food.

  - I also provide tools to navigate fitness/nutrition/food social media and how to be an educated consumer online.

- You are what you eat—this book will help you understand how and what you choose to fuel yourself with says a lot about who you are and what you believe in!

- I interview some popular creators on social media about their journeys with food/cooking. The "food side" of various social media platforms is incredibly diverse today and can consist of self-proclaimed "foodies," celebrity chefs, home chefs, and food critics, to name a few. One thing they all have in common is the value they ascribe to food, and in some cases, cooking, which they project onto the world.

PART ONE

THE ART AND CULTURE OF FOOD

Cooking Up Inspiration

Growing up in a Korean American family, I ate a lot of food that is representative of my heritage. I recall waking up on birthdays to traditional seaweed soup, helping my parents prepare for backyard barbeque parties with family and friends with Korean barbequed short ribs, and eating lettuce wraps instead of hot dogs.

Dinner at my family's house—galbi tacos!

However, my lifestyle did not always match what I consumed, since my parents did not completely fit the stereotypical immigrant "Asian parents" mold. Rather, both of my parents had come to America at a fairly early age and speak English fluently. I grew up speaking English and, to this day, still have a hard time speaking Korean or fully relating to my Korean friends and their cultural inclinations, especially their interactions with elders. However, one thing we all share is a love of Korean foods. I have found dishes have the ability to unite people, regardless of language. Furthermore, my understanding of Korean food has enabled me to foster a connection to my heritage, separate from my lived-in experiences as a Korean American.

A typical Korean meal of rice, soup, and assorted banchan

Last year, I took a trip to lead a team of high school students across South Korea, helping establish English language programs for underfunded schools. At first, it was extremely difficult to communicate with them because of my lack of fluency in Korean. For them, speaking to me was like trying to understand a toddler—slightly understandable, but mostly confusing. One of the most memorable moments was speaking with some of the students at these schools. I still remember their shock, then delight, when I relayed to them some of my favorite traditional dishes in recognizable Korean. I named some of my most adventurous food combinations, like raw squid with sesame oil, blood sausage and spicy rice cakes, and multigrain powder sticky rice cakes, similar to mochi. Despite my clumsy language skills and seemingly "Americanized" ways, my appreciation for some of Korea's most traditional dishes proved to them I was truly one of them at heart. From these interactions, I began to realize how food can be so powerful in connecting people to and across cultures.

When I visited Finland in 2019, I discovered a local outdoor market in Helsinki. The vivid colors of locally sourced produce and delectable scents of prepared seafood was a feast for my senses, and I spent hours roaming from stall to stall, learning about the cultures and customs of Finland through its food offerings and human interactions with vendors. I stopped at one stall that featured a diverse array of multicolored homemade jams.

Growing up in America, I never had a huge affinity for jams or jellies. I was not interested in these sugary options of grape or strawberry jam; I preferred my fruit in its original state best. I was drawn to this particular stand, however, because of how unique its jam flavors were, and how beautifully they were packaged, ready for consumption. Flavors like lingonberry and sea buckthorn piqued my interest, and the lady manning the stand took notice of my fascination with her products. She invited me to take a closer look and even offered samples of her favorite jams. I sampled the sea buckthorn first and was floored by its immediate tartness, a taste I had disassociated with preserved fruit. Its slight citrus flavor and layered sweetness led me to purchase one of each flavor I sampled, and I eventually brought them home to my family, who marveled at their unique yet wonderful flavor profiles. Despite them not having visited Finland, they were able to get a taste of Scandinavia from thousands of miles away.

Some of the jam offerings available at the market

The stalls at the market

The kind lady at the market who offered
me a sampling of her products

Not only did my interest in food help develop my cultural awareness, but it was a huge factor in the development of many of my interpersonal relationships. During my sophomore year of college, I balanced a heavy workload with on-campus extracurriculars, as well as a part-time internship. At times, I felt like work and school were my entire life. Despite my hectic lifestyle, I would try my best to make time to eat dinner at home with my friends or cook a meal together we could all enjoy. From baking French chestnut cakes to making baked ziti as a team effort, these memories have ingrained themselves into my feelings about cooking. Some of these nights with my apartment mates still remain my favorite memories, and the family recipes we shared helped us grow closer to each other. At times like this, cooking was an oasis, separate from all my work-related and academic anxieties.

For me, cooking is so much more than a survival mechanism.

- Cooking can represent companionship, like when my apartment mates and I prepared meals together in our tiny apartment. In fact, one of my favorite recipes—chestnut cake—actually comes from my best friend's family.

- It can be a way to help better yourself, like when I ditched fast food and takeout options to prepare my own nutritious meals at home.

- It can also represent independence, because it is a skill necessary when moving away from your family.

- It can also be educational, because one can learn so much about a different culture by the cuisine *and* the preparation methods. Cooking and food to me equals human connection and self-actualization.

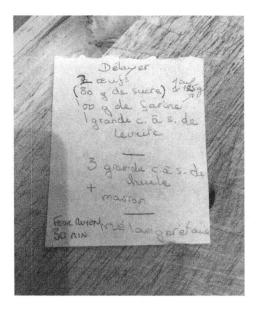

The recipe for Anaïs's family chestnut cake, handwritten and passed down through generations

Regardless of what your creative outlet may be, one thing is certain: it brings you a recognizable sense of euphoria and peace. My creative outlet is food preparation, and I love to explore how cooking can both nutritionally nourish someone and also nourish the soul.

This book is separated into two distinct parts. In the first part, I will unravel some of what I consider to be the most poignant human relationships and connections that have been facilitated by food with experiences from my life as well as subjects I interviewed. This is based on my understanding of human interaction, emotions, and sociology. In the second part, however, I will examine the phenomenon of the food landscape on social media that inhibits healthy relationships with food. In an effort to be as real as I can, some of these stories, especially those that deal with the subject of disordered eating, may be triggering, and they will have a trigger warning at the beginning of the chapter.

I hope by the end of this book, you will have gained a deeper understanding of the way *you* interact with food on a daily basis. Hopefully, you will have a clear starting point in which to change or keep some of the food habits you can identify. Food is something organisms need, but only humans have made it truly an emotional experience. If you have any special stories in your own life about food and humans, please message me on Instagram @ mendameals so I can share your stories with my small but intimate following!

Baking Bread and Breaking Bread

———

When I was in my junior year of high school, I got my driver's license. The feeling of liberation that ensued was probably a result of the beginning of what would be the rest of my life—adulthood.

Like many children, I often daydreamed about my future and what it would look like. By sixteen, I would have been invited to perform violin in New York. At eighteen, I would have graduated high school as valedictorian and been on my way to an Ivy League institution, probably Harvard. I would study abroad at twenty, graduate by twenty-one. By twenty-five, I would have my own publishing studio in New York after becoming a best-selling author of a young adult fiction series, be happily married, and have lots of animals.

In reality, I stopped seriously pursuing violin at seventeen and never applied to Harvard. I was stuck at home, quarantined because of a global pandemic for half of my twentieth year, and lost motivation for the other half. By twenty-one, I will graduate from college and face a future that feels all too uncertain.

The point is the only thing certain about your own coming-of-age story is uncertainty.

What I didn't realize as a child was food and cooking would define my adulthood. Whether that manifested itself through tumultuous arguments with my psyche concerning my elaborate food rules or cooking dinners for my parents and learning how to meal prep, food would take the center stage of Act Two of my life.

For me, one side of cooking represents a creative process in which I can express my favorite sides of myself. Some days, I am a mad scientist, experimenting with unique ingredients and testing flavor profiles against each other. Other days, I am a health nut, balancing fresh vegetables and fruits with responsible proteins. And yet other days, I feel like an innovator, replicating some of my favorite restaurant dishes with my own spin. Every part of my body is engaged when I test the bounds of my creativity, relishing in the endless possibilities I face in the kitchen. In the same way, the duality of nourishing oneself with food nutritionally and emotionally has implications on ourselves, our relationships, and the world we live in. Through the lens of food, much of our world becomes clearer and more digestible.

One of the restaurants I hope to dine at before I die is Alinea in Chicago, Illinois. Alinea is a restaurant that breaks all the rules of what fine dining should look like through its innovative food designs and interactive meals. Not only is the three-Michelin-starred restaurant known for its delicious dishes, but it is also known for its unconventional aesthetics through molecular gastronomy. In the past few years, it has also won the 2016 Outstanding Restaurant and Services awards from the James Beard Foundation and the 2006 Best Restaurant in America award by Gourmet Magazine.

For Grant Achatz, the chef and owner, dining at Alinea is both an experience and entertainment. With interactive meals that invite diners to take part in the presentation and serving of the food, Achatz displays the connection between art and food. In his book, *Games for Actors and Non-Actors*, drama theorist and Brazilian theater practitioner Augusto Boal describes the identity and role of the "spect-actor."[1] Boal explains audiences to a theater performance should never feel isolated from what they are watching. Instead, they should take some part in the action, thus becoming a spectator and an actor, or "spect-actor." Fine dining and theater are similar in the fact diners and audience members alike are paying for a performance. With fine dining, this can entail the ambience of a restaurant, that certain je ne sais quoi that differentiates it from other establishments. Alinea takes this concept literally with its eye-catching, artistic displays of food that are interactive, even at the tableside level.

Personally, the reason why this restaurant is on my bucket list is because I resonate with Achatz's philosophy that food is so much more than a nutritional unit. It can be entertainment, and even at that level, it is not one-sided. I love how Alinea breaks so many unsaid rules of fine

---

1   Augusto Boal, *Theater of the Oppressed* (New York: Theatre Communications Group, 1985), 134–136.

dining, and how it conventionally looks. In my own cooking, I carry the same philosophy with me as I feed others.

Grant Achatz: The Reimagining of Taste

Achatz grew up in a restaurant environment, working at his parents' restaurant, Achatz's Family Restaurant, even working as a cook at the age of twelve.[2] He described this restaurant as a "social gathering place in the community" that nourished its patrons through its food offerings.[3] This humble restaurant focused primarily on simple food, not aesthetics, a mold Achatz was determined to defy. For him, food was so much more than a basic necessity for life—it was an art form. After graduating from the Culinary Institute of America, Achatz worked for various restaurants, the most prominent being the French Laundry in Northern California. Working at the French Laundry shaped Achatz's philosophy about unconventional tastes and presentations. After working under Thomas Keller, head chef at the French Laundry, he decided to part ways and soon became the chef of Trio, where he executed innovative dishes like the Truffle Explosion, a ravioli dish that was filled with a liquid instead of a traditional solid filling. After long work weeks, Achatz began to gain acclaim in the restaurant world for his work at Trio, even earning the Rising Star Chef award from the James Beard Foundation in 2003.[4]

---

2   D.T. Max, "A Man of Taste: A chef with cancer fights to save his tongue," *New Yorker* (Web*)*, May 12, 2008.

3   Max, *New Yorker*.

4   "Awards for Alinea," Alinea Restaurant Group, accessed January 1, 2021.

In May of 2005, Achatz made another departure, this time with his own venture concept—Alinea, a minimalist restaurant in Chicago that emphasized relatively unexplored cooking methods of molecular gastronomy. During this time, Achatz began to develop lesions in his mouth, an inconvenience some medical experts initially dismissed as a side effect of Achatz's long work hours and dedication to his craft. Although Achatz felt some discomfort, he continued to pursue his dream of establishing his own restaurant.

Alinea was met with much critical acclaim in its initial years, and was even given the title of the best restaurant in the United States of America. The following months were typified by a hullabaloo of excitement, with television program appearances, cookbook deals, new restaurant ventures, and even more acclaim. Despite the scientific methods employed to prepare the dishes, Achatz described the Alinea experience as an "art form, ... [which] is in many ways the opposite of science ... we do a good job of evoking emotion though food, and that's ... our focus, our perspective."[5]

In the midst of this period, Achatz's mouth condition worsened, and he employed new, temporary methods to deal with it. Some methods were more precise than others, like a professionally fitted mouthguard, but others were scrappier, like pushing a piece of chewing gum between the lesions and his teeth. By early 2007, the lesions were not the major source of discomfort, as a tumor had developed and swollen his mouth. Because of the difficulty that ensued from simply speaking and eating, Achatz's physical symptoms worsened, including

5   Max, *New Yorker.*

weight loss. The same year, as he sought out remedies for this discomfort, he was diagnosed with stage four tongue cancer. At the time, the only viable treatment was a partial removal of his tongue that would leave him with limited taste. For the average person, this was a dire situation to be in—losing one of the five senses would change the trajectory of anyone's life. For Achatz, a renowned chef and leading figure in the culinary world, this prognosis was earth-shattering. Food was his entire life and his purpose; how could a chef who could not taste continue his craft to the best of his ability?

The University of Chicago had been working on a clinical trial procedure for head and neck cancer patients in late stages. Achatz was determined to fight for his sense of taste and, after a few tests, began treatment, which included vigorous rounds of chemotherapy. Although it was effective in killing the cancerous cells, Achatz's physical side effects were drastic, including falling weight and a temporary complete loss of taste.

After the grueling months that followed this loss, Achatz began to slowly regain his sense of taste, starting with the ability to identify the element of sweetness. He described the process as that of a "newborn," as he started to experience flavor for what felt like the first time. With his understanding of the flavor as a thirty-two-year-old chef, he was able to reimagine his knowledge of food with this new visceral perspective of how flavors could be reimagined through the building blocks of taste.[6]

---

6   Terry Gross and Grant Achatz, "Grant Achatz: The Chef Who Couldn't Taste," August 29, 2011, produced by National Public Radio, interview, MP3 audio, 37:02.

When asked about this entire experience, Achatz simply says, "*I don't recommend it, but...I think it made me a better chef.*"[7]

Cooking, like many other creative outlets, is a form of artistic expression. And, like most art, it romanticizes life and makes the ugly sides of life palatable. Just as a beautiful painting should be shared and admired, food is the physical representation of my creative freedom, and its reception by others is their interpretation of my creation. Although my seared scallops in caper butter sauce may remind me of events, like my parents' anniversary dinner during quarantine, it may remind the person I am cooking for about a scuba diving trip in the Caribbean.

Although our individual understandings of food are personalized to us, they also connect us. Food connects people in a way no other art form does, simply due to its interactive and highly personal nature. Whether it looks like catching up with a friend over coffee, taking a cooking class with a significant other, or baking treats for a fundraising cause, food connects all of us—no matter where we are or what language we speak.

My understanding of global food cultures primarily stems from my diverse group of friends and people I have surrounded myself with in the past. Because of the people I have interacted with in life, I have been exposed to new foods and cooking techniques, invaluable gifts that still stay with me today. Relating to others through their food traditions or cultures is something that can easily bond two people and break an awkwardness that may be initially present. Showing interest in other people's

---

7   Gross and Achatz, NPR, 37:40.

knowledge about their food or cuisine also has the effect of showing someone you are interested in what makes them, since food says a lot about who you are.

The assortment of dim sum I enjoyed at the iconic Tim Ho Wan in its original location in Hong Kong

In addition to my personal human interactions, I have also been very blessed to travel to many countries known for their cuisine and learned much about how different food cultures can shape cultural beliefs and traditions. At the same time, I have noticed how food can serve as a great introduction or icebreaker when in a new country or city.

An egg tart from Tai Cheong Bakery, a Hong Kong institution, known for its Hong Kong-style egg tarts

Pan-fried and steamed soup dumplings, also from Hong Kong

Cultural Food Fluency

In the summer of 2019, I traveled to South Korea and stayed with my great-aunt and uncle, whom I had met only once before. I didn't know what to expect and worried about my lack of Korean fluency as I counted down the days until I would meet them at the train station.

Upon meeting them, my fears were slightly confirmed—the awkwardness was exacerbated by our lack of a fluent, shared language. As we drove to their apartment from the station, my great-aunt started to ask questions about America, such as what a day would look like for me at home. Without thinking much of this, I mentioned how I love to start my day with an iced Americano and a small breakfast of toast, yogurt, or fruit before I walked to class. Once we arrived at their apartment, I was surprised by how they had meticulously planned for my arrival, with a personal refrigerator filled with "American" snacks and water, a mirror, a bedside table, and a bed.

After eight hours of nonstop travel from South Korea's rural south to Seoul, its capital city, I was exhausted and quickly fell asleep. The next morning, I awoke to my great-aunt knocking on my room door with a tray of my favorite breakfast foods. Not only did she wake up early to go grocery shopping for me, but she also purchased all of my favorite "American" breakfast items I typically enjoyed at home.

Even if we didn't speak the same language, she found another way to connect with me. After breaking the initial discomfort with food, I felt less self-conscious about my poor Korean-speaking skills and tried to connect with her through the language she was most comfortable.

Eventually, my great-aunt and I became very close that summer. I kept her company as we babysat her grandchildren, she showed me some of her favorite landmarks in Seoul, and I practiced my Korean daily with her through conversation. That summer, I developed my Korean language skills remarkably and learned how paramount language can be to personal connection.

A simple lunch of cold noodles (naengmyeon) and various banchan prepared for me by my great-aunt

A dinner at my great-aunt's apartment of abalone jook, or rice
porridge, and various leafy greens to self-assemble wraps

As a Korean American growing up in America, I often
felt isolated from my Korean roots. Although I had visited South Korea with my family when I was a child, and
once again only a year prior to this trip with my mom,
I had never felt an instant connection with the country.
Whether it was my physical appearance that isolated
me from other Koreans or my own inability to naturally
communicate, South Korea was a distant vacation spot
for me, not necessarily another home.

From this trip, however, I grew a new appreciation
for a place I really got to understand. Although it was my
first time in South Korea without at least some members

of my direct family, my solo travels allowed me to really see the country for what it was.

From early morning bus rides to the city center to mandu tastings at Namdaemun Market, the city came alive to me. Although I may not have been able to fluently order my favorite dishes at restaurants and food stalls, the tastes were already known to me. My appreciation for this familiarity only deepened when I saw my own speaking skills improve when ordering alone. One of my favorite ways to observe the city was in solitude, alone at a small stand or restaurant, enjoying my own meal. Oftentimes, I would notice things I normally wouldn't have in a group. Whether they were small interactions with groups, couples sharing bingsoo, or strangers walking outside in groups, I always learned more about the city through these pockets of time.

Mandu from Namdaemun Market in Seoul, South Korea

My favorite Korean soup, samgyetang, which is Cornish hen simmered in aromatics like ginger and ginseng, is said to have healing properties. I enjoyed this chicken soup at a small rural town in southern South Korea.

Purple corn harvested in southern South Korea by a group of local elders

A close-up of the glutinous purple corn

By the end of the trip, I had learned an important lesson: an underrated way to get to know someone is through food. It is quite fitting that when I left, my great-aunt picked up some of my favorite dumplings at a stand near her apartment to eat for breakfast.

Today, South Korea has a special place in my heart, and Seoul in particular feels like a second home to me. Rectifying the cultural damage I had self-inflicted started with finding peace with a physical location and through food.

In the same way food can connect families and individuals with their roots, food can be a connecting factor in which an entire relationship is based on.

I met one of my best friends, Anaïs Connelly, in 2018, after we decided to live together in our freshman apartment-style dormitory with six other girls. When we initially met at a USC acceptance event, the awkwardness between us was palpable. Coming from two radically different places (Irvine vs. Manhattan), we didn't have much to talk about. By the end of the day, we had both internalized the fact we probably would not be close friends. Although there was no tension or verbal agreement, we assumed our lifestyles were just too different to ever be more than acquaintances.

When the semester started in the fall, we both struggled with two things: finding someone to go to the dining hall with and understanding our cultural identities. As my roommates and I shared meals together at the dining hall, I found myself letting go of a lot of the insecurities about who I was and how I fit into USC. Through the meals we shared together, we shared our stories, our lives, our hopes and dreams, and our fears. Although we had a mutual disgust for some of the food items at the dining hall, one of the main ways our group came together was through spending time together over a meal at the dining hall.

But for Anaïs and I, only our social anxiety problems had been solved with establishing our friend group. One problem still remained—understanding our heritage and identity. As we spent more time together, our friendship became more defined by the similar feelings we had regarding our roots. As children of immigrants, we both struggled with idealizing and embracing our roots. One night, Anaïs shared how she used to be ashamed of her culture growing up in the American public school system, where anything outside the normal was "weird." She quickly dismissed her experiences as nonissues, simply based on the fact she is white. I remember immediately defending her against herself, making sure she understood her pain and struggle to reclaim her culture were valid, no matter what her race was. Although it should go without saying certain groups of people have faced more oppressive circumstances than others, we as a society should never dismiss one person's experiences by comparing them to another.

One summer, Anaïs visited my childhood home and spent a week with me. The day she left, my mom baked some of her special blueberry muffins and offered some to us. Knowing Anaïs came from a French background and was picky about her baked goods, I quickly explained the texture of these muffins would be very different than what she was used to, since my mom used Mochiko, a sweet rice flour, instead of all-purpose. Expecting she wouldn't like my mom's mochi muffins, I reassured her she did not have to try the muffins if she didn't want to. Despite my warning, Anaïs gingerly tasted one and quickly devoured the muffin. My mom's expectant expression turned to one of delight and, upon request, she packed a box of muffins for Anaïs to take home with her. I was shocked Anaïs genuinely enjoyed the blueberry mochi muffins, yet appreciative of her willingness to try a different food item I grew up eating.

Mom's Mochi Muffins

Ingredients:

- glutinous rice flour (not rice flour!)
  - preferred brand: Mochiko
- 3 eggs
- lemon (for zest)
- salt
- cane sugar
  - optional for topping: turbinado sugar, or raw sugar (coarse)
- 2 cups of warm milk (or canned coconut milk)
- blueberries
- 1 stick of butter
- baking powder
- vanilla extract
- sugar

Steps:

1.) The night before baking, pour one-fourth cup of sugar (more or less depending on how sweet you like it) over a cup of blueberries and let sit covered overnight in the refrigerator.

2.) The next day, stir the sugar and blueberry mixture until well-combined. The blueberries should still retain their general circular shape.

3.) Preheat oven to 375 degrees Fahrenheit.

4.) In a large bowl, combine three cups of glutinous rice flour with a half teaspoon of salt, zest of half a lemon, and one teaspoon of baking powder.

5.) In a smaller vessel, combine a half cup of sugar with softened butter until creamed together. Add warm milk, room temperature eggs, and a teaspoon of vanilla extract.

6.) Add wet ingredients to dry and mix until barely combined. Once combined, let sit for ten minutes.

7.) After sitting, softly fold in blueberry mixture (you can also use a different choice of mix-ins, such as dark chocolate chips, coconut flakes, sweet adzuki beans, or even omit the blueberries completely—just add more sugar).

8.) Pour mixture into a greased or lined muffin tin pan until half full. Top with turbinado sugar.

9.) Bake for twenty to twenty-five minutes, depending on how well done or soft you prefer your mochi muffins.

As the school year started after the summer, Anaïs and I started to connect our friendship to our shared passion of cooking and baking for others. One day, she received a care package in the mail from her parents. In this package were two cans of a mysterious puree, imported from France. That night, Anaïs used these cans of sweetened chestnut puree to bake a simple chestnut cake. After she dusted the top of the circular, warm, golden-brown crust with powdered sugar, she shyly offered it to my apartment mates and me. As the scent of the toasty, caramel-like sweetness wafted through the apartment, I emerged from my room to taste her chestnut cake. Just like I had warned her over the summer that she might not like my mom's muffins, she warned me that it might not match my palate. But upon my first bite of the cake, still warm from the oven, I was in love. The perfect softness yet slight crustiness from the edges of the cake melded together in my mouth as the incredible roasted chestnut flavor met my taste buds. To this day, Anaïs' family recipe for French chestnut cake is my favorite baked good.

Anaïs' and my apartment pantry and living room in 2020

Anaïs' Chestnut Cake

Ingredients:

- 2 eggs
- 80g of sugar
- 100g of flour
- 1 large tablespoon of baking powder
- 3 tablespoons of oil
- 250g creme de marrons (chestnut puree)
- recommended brand: Clement Faugier vanilla chestnut spread

Steps:

1.) Combine eggs, sugar, flour, and baking powder.

2.) In a separate bowl, mix oil and creme de marrons.

3.) Mix it all together and bake in the oven for thirty minutes at 350 degrees Fahrenheit. Serve with powdered sugar lightly dusted on top of the cake after flipping.

A focal point of our relationship is encouraging the growth of our cultural identities. The main way we help each other do this is through shared meals. A similarity between the two of us is our love for not only food, but also cooking. By learning our own family recipes and preparing them for the two of us, we have increased our cultural knowledge base about our own culture and each other's.

Now, Anais and I are raising an herb garden in our small apartment. Despite quarantine, we do our best to keep ourselves busy and, given our shared love of cooking, we decided to start gardening ingredients we could readily incorporate in our home-cooked meals. One of our favorite aromatic plants to use in cooking is our basil plant, which we use in our Italian and Thai-inspired dinners, like pesto pasta and yellow curry. Although pesto sauce can be very convenient when store-bought, homemade pesto has a greater depth of richness and is more customizable to one's palate, which results in the best pesto *you* will try.

Anaïs' and my humble herb garden

Apartment Pesto

Ingredients:

- 3 handfuls of fresh basil
- Better Than Bouillon chicken stock concentrate
- 4 cloves of garlic
- raw pine nuts
- olive oil

Steps:

1.) Pick three handfuls worth of fresh basil, and after washing them, place in a blender cup or food processor.

2.) Add one tablespoon of Better Than Bouillon chicken concentrate.

3.) Toast one-third cup of pine nuts on low heat in a small saucepan.

4.) Once browned and oil starts to release, add it to the blending vessel.

5.) Add two glugs of extra virgin olive oil with garlic.

6.) Blend.

7.) Serve over pasta, or carb of choice.

8.) Add cream/salt if desired, but I prefer it without because you can really taste the garlic-y, herb-y goodness. When serving, grate Parmigiano-Reggiano over top and add a few raw pine nuts.

Food is so much more than just nutrients and taste. It is simultaneously art and scientific discovery. It is the very fiber of human connection, a solitary or shared experience that recolors our imaginings of the world. Through our physical senses, we can unlock the intangible: our emotions, memories, and future experiences.

The Three Fs: Food, Friends, Family

———

Like a good inside joke, family recipes can evoke a sense of belonging and nostalgia. They stimulate memories despite how simple or complex they may be. Despite how unconventional some family recipes are, for at least one person, these meals are priceless. Personally, some of my favorite family recipes are loose interpretations of different cuisines from around the world.

The phrase "family recipe" should not simply entail one's biological family, however. Let's do an exercise together. Close your eyes and think about your close circle of people, whether they be your nuclear family or your best friends. After you envision them, think about the way you interact with each other through the context of food. Do you have a favorite cuisine or restaurant? Does a specific snack brand or unconventional ingredient bring up inside jokes? Regardless of how often you see them, you probably have strong memories relating them and some sort of meal. Identifying and isolating these moments will lead to a greater appreciation for each other as well as whatever meal you will share with them in the future. Why? Because these memories serve as key ingredients in a meal that not only nourishes the body, but also the soul.

Foods can be extremely polarizing. People love to debate, so it's no surprise how passionately some will express their love for or disgust of foods like olives, pickles, or ketchup, to name a few. One food that falls into this category is one of Korea's most famous offerings—kimchi.

A traditional Korean meal with two types of kimchi banchan, one cubed radish (mu) kimchi and one traditional napa cabbage kimchi

Kimchi is a spicy, fermented cabbage typically served as a "banchan," or side dish, to other foods. However, kimchi can be served in many different ways and variations: cold, as a base for soup, as a cucumber side dish instead of cabbage. Since it is such a versatile food, the possibilities are truly endless. One of my favorite variations of kimchi is "kimchi-bokkeum," or stir-fried kimchi. My family likes to add water, a teaspoon of sugar, and a tablespoon of reduced sodium soy sauce to amplify the flavor. Although not traditional, my sister and I like to add kimchi-bokkeum to our childhood favorite meal, grilled cheese. In this way, my family is able to enjoy our recipes that are representations of who we are as a family.

Kimchi Grilled Cheese

Ingredients:

- kimchi
- bread of choice (I like sourdough)
- Parmigiano-Reggiano
- mozzarella
- light soy sauce
- brown sugar
- olive oil (avocado oil and butter are okay)
- optional: sesame seeds, sesame oil

Steps:

1.) Rinse the kimchi a little bit with water so the juice is diluted, but reserve this liquid. This is to reduce extra saltiness and act as a braising liquid for the kimchi.

2.) Stir-fry it on low with a tablespoon of oil. Add soy sauce, sugar, and the braising liquid. The amount of liquid should not fully cover the bottom of the pan.

3.) Cook until caramelized and most of the liquid is reduced significantly. The kimchi should not be very wet, nor should it be dry. At this stage, the kimchi should take on a darker, reddish color and become more wilted. At this point, it is called "kimchi-bok-keum," or stir-fried kimchi.

4.) Once caramelized, add a teaspoon of sesame oil to the kimchi.

5.) After one minute, turn off heat and sprinkle sesame seeds over top of the kimchi.

6.) Toast two slices of bread (sourdough is my favorite) with cheese evenly dispersed on top of the two slices (use a toaster oven or oven).

7.) Once the bread is toasted and cheese melted, place kimchi-bokkeum on top of one slice of bread and put the two pieces together. You can also slather butter on the outside facing slices and pan-fry until cheese is completely melted.

8.) Slice diagonally to serve.

Something so unique about the foodscape in the United States is the separation of the casual/rustic and the formal/elevated. We usually correlate home-cooking and family recipes with the former, when in reality, this opposing binary exists in the same way many systems in America do—to bolster a certain industry. The devaluation of home-cooked meals is easy when it exists almost in a separate sphere from "outside food," or food cooked in a kitchen other than your own. While restaurant cuisine should be respected in its own right, it should not serve as a binary to cooking at home.

A home-cooked meal of braised kimchi tofu with avocado and wild rice

---

Take one food phenomenon celebrated at many levels of American society—the potluck. When we think about American food culture, my mind instantly goes to holidays. In my family (and many others), holidays like Thanksgiving, Christmas, and Easter all center around the quintessentially American potluck. Before we delve into the intersection of family and human connection, let's take a brief look at the history of the word "potluck," according to foodtimeline.org.

Potluck Timeline[8]

1592: The word "potluck" is used in print for the very first time in England. Its original definition is very literal, with the first half of the word, "pot," referring to a meal being cooked (usually by someone else), and "luck," meaning taking a chance with the aforementioned, what is being cooked ("pot").

Late 1800s: The "luck" and "chance" aspect of "potluck" is emphasized, with a more specific description of a meal shared in which each attendee brings a dish. The word "supper" usually follows this use of the word.

2011: The government of Minnesota passes the "Church Lady Law" in light of the growing popularity of potlucks at religious functions. The law states that although faith-based organizations do not have to undergo a health inspection, at least one potluck contributor must have "adequate food safety training."

Today: When the word "potluck" is used, it means each guest brings a food item to a special occasion, like a company dinner party, a holiday dinner, a celebratory event, or a picnic.[9]

It is important to note there is an alternate theory, that the word is derived from the Native American ritual of "potlatch."[10] Potlatches were ceremonial feasts that revolved around gift giving, guests, and speeches.

8   Chris Wells. "The Potluck: A Native American Thanksgiving Tradition?" The Houston Museum of Natural Science: Beyond Bones (blog), November 16, 2016.

9   Lisa Bramen. "Good Night and Good Potluck," *Smithsonian Magazine*, May 25, 2010.

10   Wells, *Beyond Bones*.

The potlatch was most common in the mid-nineteenth century to the early twentieth century, especially with Native Americans located near the northwest Pacific coast. This ceremony was as much a feast as it was a social custom that solidified and improved the status of people.

Not many countries, with the exception of the United States, partake in feasts; other celebrations around the world mainly place the burden of providing food on the host. Not only is the concept of a potluck representative of American individualism, but it also sets the social atmosphere for guests to connect with each other in a convenient yet exciting manner. In my family, Thanksgiving is a time when I get to see my extended family and indulge in a delicious variety of dishes that is not unlike my family—large, diverse, and unique.

A group photo with my paternal family at one Thanksgiving

This past fall was actually the first time I didn't celebrate Thanksgiving with my extended family due to the global pandemic. In addition, because my family was moving out of my childhood home, things were pretty chaotic, meaning our Thanksgiving dinner consisted of takeout from our favorite Korean restaurant after moving boxes back and forth for the entire day. Thanksgiving Day had truly worn us out, both physically and emotionally.

After finally settling on a restaurant, picking up our order, and arguing over how much to tip, the tension in the car driving back home was palpable. This was definitely not the Thanksgiving I was used to, and it felt like all of my favorite parts about the holiday—the social connection and human interaction, the diverse and plentiful array of home-cooked meats and side dishes, the feeling of going to sleep on a full but completely satisfied belly and heart—were robbed from me. As I passive-aggressively set the table and unboxed the food, my dad asked me to say a prayer before we ate. As I hesitated before begrudgingly listing what I was grateful for in the form of a prayer, I reflected on this unconventional Thanksgiving. Despite the complications, conflicts, and chaos that had ensued earlier in the day, the mere reflection of gratitude I verbalized before sharing a meal with my family made me appreciate the food and quality time I spent with my family even more.

To return to our discourse about the origins of the American potluck, I ask, how does the humble potluck achieve the same result of gratitude in a group setting?

When you picture a potluck, you probably visualize a fairly large gathering of people. These people may be extended family, friends, co-workers, or even complete strangers. Regardless of how they are related, they have all contributed a part of themselves into the main event—the meal. A potluck dinner is typically disjointed and non-cohesive, and that is the beauty of it. What you cook is who you are.

Brittani Lancaster—Pie Slices of Me

Since body positive influencer Brittani Lancaster was in seventh grade, she has consistently made the same dessert for her family's Thanksgiving and Christmas dinners: apple pie.

For as long as she could remember, Brittani remembered her mom hosting holiday dinners. In the midst of a particularly busy holiday season, (twelve-year-old?) Brittani watched as her mother frantically planned appetizers, allocated baking tasks, prepared salads, and roasted meats. When the realization no one had signed up to make dessert dawned on her, Brittani jumped at the opportunity to help. The worst-case scenario, she thought, was there just wouldn't be dessert.

She meticulously followed a recipe she found in a cookbook in her mom's house and baked her first Thanksgiving apple pie. To her delight, the pie was an absolute hit. The next year, there was no question who would be baking dessert.

The rest of the story continues, as Brittani's family expects her now signature apple pie to make an appearance each year. Not only does this dish bring Brittani's family enjoyment, but it also brings her a sense of absolute happiness to bake. For her, baking pie is not just a mindless activity; it is an expression of joy and appreciation for family that transports her to the holidays.

In the same way Brittani thinks about her family when baking, her family thinks of her when eating pie. Sometimes, her relatives will send her photos of a slice of apple pie they have at an event, with the message, "Wish it was your apple pie."

A lemon tart with Italian meringue baked by Anaïs

As humans, we have a special ability to ascribe sentimental value to seemingly meaningless things. Food is one of these things. But why do we correlate food with emotions and memories? As physical beings, we rely on our five sense to perceive the world around us. If you think about it, each of these senses, whether it be sight, physical touch, smell, taste, or hearing, helps us immortalize memories. Think about a place from your past that holds strong memories for you, then mentally (or physically) fill in the blanks.

When I think of (place), I can smell _____.

When I think of (place), I can hear _____.

When I think of (place), I can visualize _____.

When I think of (place), I remember the taste of _____.

When I think of (place), I remember how _____ feels.

Here's mine:

When I think of Disneyland, I can smell the chlorinated water of Splash Mountain.

When I think of Disneyland, I can hear the theme park music, the rolling of strollers, the laughing and crying of children, and the roaring of rollercoasters making their final descent.

When I think of Disneyland, I can visualize the long lines of my favorite rides.

When I think of Disneyland, I remember the taste of the piping hot cinnamon churros I begged my dad to buy for me.

When I think of Disneyland, I remember how the cool water splashing in my face while riding Grizzly Bear Rapids felt.

Does it surprise you how much you remember this place through the isolation of senses? This is why we think about our exes when we hear a certain song, feel nostalgic when we eat our favorite childhood snacks, and crave our parent's cooking when we are homesick.

So, to the question, "Why do we intertwine foods with our memories and emotions?" I would answer we perceive food through taste, and it is through taste we are transported to our past. When we are transported to our past, we are able to express gratitude—an emotion we then come to correlate with food.

Tiffany Hsieh—Memorializing Meals

I interviewed Tiffany Hsieh, who graduated from the University of California, Los Angeles, with a Bachelor of Science in nutrition in 2019. For Tiffany, food plays a central part in not only her personal life, but also her academic career. Although she entered UCLA as a freshman planning to major in biology, one class, Nutrition Through the Life Cycle, shifted her perspective on nutrition. Through this class, she realized how nutrition plays a central role in each stage of life, even from the beginnings with the breastmilk of a mother to her child.

During one year of her nutrition studies, Tiffany lived abroad in Italy, where she experienced the culture through inarguably the best lens possible: carbs. As someone who loves Italian food, she was in heaven, sampling different pasta shapes and sauces each week. When she reflects on her experiences in Italy, one specific dish comes to mind.

Even today, when Tiffany sees a photo of carbonara, she is transported to her stay in Italy. She recalls a specific restaurant she enjoyed this dish in and sometimes still even dreams about the pasta from this restaurant.

For her, food is a sensory experience—it quite literally jogs her memory. But Tiffany's memorialization of her favorite meals does not end with her travels. Since food is so central to her life, many of her cherished moments with her close friends and family revolve around shared meals.

For some, cooking is a complete chore. It is a responsibility that is usually unduly placed on one person in a family. When Tiffany talks about cooking as a bonding activity, she focuses on the distribution of responsibility and connection. Just like potlucks, cooking together removes the burden of tasks that can be stressful and reallocates it to everyone. Communal cooking also gives each person significance, as individuals can pinpoint exactly what they have done to make the dish in question.

The Currency of Love

Last year marked my grandmother's eightieth birthday. Although my family usually celebrates birthdays with a strawberry cream cake from our local Korean bakery, one of my mom's closest friends, Junghee, made two rice cakes for my grandmother for this birthday. In Korean culture, rice cakes, or "dduk," are traditional cakes used to celebrate Korean holidays like Korean Thanksgiving (Chuseok), events like birthdays, or an infant's first hundred days.

One of the cakes we will typically get for a Korean birthday or celebration. This one is the blueberry yogurt cake from Paris Baguette I had for my twentieth birthday in quarantine.

A cake made of a base of steamed rice flour is not baked like a traditional birthday cake. In fact, it doesn't even require an oven, since it is steamed over a pot. Making the cake is also a tedious process, and with the exception of a select few counters at a Korean grocery store, they are not readily available for sale. They also do not keep well and must be enjoyed the same day. Junghee woke up that morning at 6:00 a.m. to make a blueberry steamed rice cake for my mom to take to her mom. Although my grandmother usually doesn't eat dessert, she loved the gesture and remarked that the cake reminded her of her younger days. For my grandmother, that dish reminded her of what it was like to celebrate an occasion in a traditional Korean way.

My grandmother, Okja Kim, immigrated to the United States of America in 1983 with five young kids in tow. Three years prior, my grandfather immigrated to set up a life for his family with his liquor store business. When my grandmother arrived in America after taking care of her children and mother-in-law for over a decade, she immediately knew what she had to do. After working long hours alongside my grandfather at Harry's Liquor Store, she came home to five hungry mouths. Despite her inability to understand English fluently, she studied the language during her very limited free time. However, she always prioritized the needs of her kids, who loved art and music. To make sure her children had as many resources as they needed to succeed, she lived to work for her family. Currently, my grandmother understands some English, but is definitely more comfortable in Korean. I think this perfectly explains the sacrifices she had to make for the betterment of the Kim family.

Although she has lived in America for almost thirty years, she never had the privilege of becoming accustomed to American life and culture. Rather, she was just thrown in, displaced from her home and the familiarity of South Korea.

Thus, the cakes Junghe had made were particularly significant, as they represented a comfort reminiscent of her roots.

As a child, I often wondered what my grandma was thinking. I often watched as she quietly prepared meals for my grandpa, and even my family when we lived with them for a year in my childhood. I remember complaining about her rice, which was always cooked with black beans. Although these black beans, or kkong, were extremely healthy and nutritionally dense, they tasted dry and bitter to my young palate.

My grandfather and grandmother in their yard in
Southern California

As I helped my grandma clear the table after dinner, I would look at my grandmother with uncertainty as she threw out the black beans I had left in my rice bowl before washing it. Unlike my parents, who would force me to finish my plate, my grandma never said a word. She never nagged me or made me feel uncomfortable with who I was or my decisions. As a naturally quiet and introverted person, she carried herself with a gentle presence, yet a seemingly impenetrable exterior I didn't understand.

Grandma's Rice:

Ingredients:

- Korean black beans
- white rice
- mixed grain multicolor sweet rice

Steps:

1.) Rinse a half cup of black beans and one cup of sweet rice, soak overnight in the refrigerator.

2.) The next day, rinse one and a half cups of white rice and drain before combining both kinds of rice and the beans in either a rice cooker or small saucepan.

3.) Pour filtered water over the grains and beans until about three-fourths of an inch of water sit over top the rice.

4.) Follow directions on rice cooker and make sure to set to the sweet rice or brown rice setting to account for the extra water. If using the stovetop method, set on medium-high heat until it comes to a rolling boil.

5.) Once the water is boiling, turn down the heat to low and cover for twelve to fifteen minutes.

6.) Rice is ready when it can be fluffed with a fork and no water is visible. Once it is at this stage, cover with the lid and let sit and steam for at least five minutes.

My grandpa, on the other hand, was the exact opposite. With his boisterous personality and warm demeanor that made my cousins and I giggle at his jokes even without knowing Korean, my grandfather was an open book. He thrived in social situations and, with his large group of similarly extroverted friends, he was the epitome of everything my grandmother was not.

After I started to take learning the Korean language seriously, I decided to practice as much as possible with my grandmother. At the time, I remember hearing my friends speak about their close relationships with their own grandparents. I, on the other hand, had never even met my late paternal grandfather, and although I had a close relationship with my paternal grandmother, my young age and lack of Korean fluency inhibited our relationship from fully growing before she passed away a few years ago. Although I had hated going to Korean school on Saturdays in elementary school, I decided to take the Korean language seriously in my freshman year of college. After visiting Korea and realizing how alienated I was to a whole other side of myself, I felt an urgency in my soul to discover what seemed like a whole new world. In addition, learning Korean would help me communicate with my grandparents, and as their granddaughter, I felt compelled to learn their stories and pass them on to generations after me.

I could hear the delight in my grandparents' voice as I called them one day and spoke to them in clear, coherent Korean sentences. "Is this really Sae-hyun?" they gleefully asked as I proudly shared my learnings to them. As I consumed more and more Korean media, Korean came to me much more easily, and my relationship with my grandparents started to take hold.

During the summer of 2020, amidst the COVID-19 pandemic, I stayed with my grandparents for a week with my mom in Torrance, California, as my grandma struggled with bouts of depression. Given her remarkable life, one in which she had sacrificed all her needs for her family, it makes sense at times she would struggle with her mental health later in life. During this time, I began to see my grandma's strength, as she was determined to overcome yet another struggle in her life. As we spent the week together, I started cooking meals for my grandparents to enjoy. After being stuck at home for almost four months at that point, my grandparents were eager to eat my creations. I remember using fresh vegetables from my grandpa's expansive garden of produce and unique spices and seasonings from my grandma's spice cabinet to create new dishes that would suit our palates.

As we shared these meals at the very dinner table I had stubbornly refused to eat black beans in rice years ago, I was struck by the realization food had shaped the majority of my relationship with my grandparents. Although my learnings of Korean definitely bolstered my relationship with them, it was through food they expressed love to me, and now vice versa. As my grandpa ate my cherry tomato pasta, sourced with ingredients from his garden, he remarked in Korean, "My granddaughter is all grown-up now."

Grandpa's Garden Tomato Sauce:

Ingredients:

- cherry tomatoes
- olive oil
- brown or white onion
- garlic

- thyme
- crushed red pepper flakes
- fresh basil
- Parmigiano-Reggiano (optional)

Steps:

1.) Chop and peel onion, add to a pan on medium-high heat with olive oil. Add smashed garlic cloves (about three).

2.) Once onions are starting to caramelize and garlic is brown, add more olive oil and turn heat to low.

3.) Add two sprigs of thyme and infuse for two minutes.

4.) Put washed cherry tomatoes in pan, slightly turning up heat. Once you can hear popping noises, pour up to one cup of water into pan and cover.

5.) Lower heat and simmer. Tomatoes are ready when they burst when lightly stirred.

6.) Uncover and keep on low heat for two minutes.

7.) Salt and sugar to taste.

8.) Serve with freshly grated Parmigiano-Reggiano cheese and torn basil over polenta cakes, pasta, or crusty bread.

As virtual school started that coming fall and I moved into my apartment in Los Angeles, I committed myself fully to school and work, eager to get back into the fast-paced routine of things after five months of quarantining with my family in Irvine. However, after a few weeks passed, I started to miss the time I had spent with my family over those five months. Although they seemed never-ending at the time, living life as if time had stood still held a certain comfort. As I spoke with my grandparents on the phone, I had an idea to deliver some of their favorite foods to them and eat dinner with them.

After getting a negative COVID test, I drove to Koreatown's Ham Ji Park, a Korean restaurant that specializes in pork dishes. Their most popular offerings are gamjatang, a hearty pork soup with huge chunks of tender meat swimming in a spiced broth with potatoes and dwejigalibi, or barbequed pork ribs. Both are Korean specialties and are not commonly made at home because of the extensive preparation and difficulty that goes into these dishes. As my grandparents had been quarantined for almost six months at that point, I decided to pick up some food to eat at their home together. As I arrived, I was greeted by my grandparents even before I got out of the car. As my grandpa helped me carry in the food, I could feel my grandparents' genuine excitement, not for the food, but because I had come to visit. As we shared the meal, my grandparents asked me about my life. Though sharing meals is common in my family, this particular instance remains one of my favorite memories, as my relationship with my grandparents had grown along with me.

Sharing a carryout meal from Ham Ji Park with my grandparents

Before I left, my grandma gave me a huge bag of Honeycrisp apples to take home with me. When I told her I couldn't possibly eat all those apples before they went bad, she said, "Take it for your apartment mates! They'll eat them!"

That week, I made an apple compote with twelve remaining apples. When my friends came over that night, I decided to serve them apple hotcakes, or cast-iron-griddled, thick pancakes filled and topped with the luscious apple compote and cinnamon. These apple hotcakes were the highlight of the night and are a dish now forever immortalized in our collective memory.

Movie Night Apple Hotcakes:

Ingredients:

Apple Compote:

- Honeycrisp apples (enough to fill ¾ of your cooking vessel)
- brown sugar
- cinnamon
- nutmeg
- water
- apple cider vinegar or lemon juice

Hotcake batter:

- wheat flour
- arrowroot starch
- lightly salted butter
- water or nut milk

Optional:

- unsweetened coconut yogurt
- cinnamon
- maple syrup

Steps:

1.) Core, peel, and cube apples and fill a pot three-fourths of the way full.

2.) Add enough water to cover one-fourth to half of the pot. Simmer on low until bubbling.

3.) Once bubbling, add brown sugar to taste. (I like to add no more than one-third cup of sugar, since the apples themselves are already sweet, and heat brings out more sweetness.)

4.) Add spices to taste and cover. Once sugar is dissolved with the steam, stir before adding the juice of a lemon (half of a lemon is good for eight apples) or apple cider vinegar (adjust to taste, balance sweetness with acid).

5.) Simmer until apples partially break apart when stirred. Put on low heat and stir until texture is chunky but broken down.

6.) Turn off heat and set aside, covered.

7.) Prepare the hotcake batter. This recipe would yield about three to four hotcakes.

8.) Put one cup of wheat flour and three tablespoons of arrowroot starch in a bowl. Add one half cup of nut milk or water.

9.) After combining (don't overmix), add another half cup of apple compote to the base.

10.) Butter a pan on medium heat. When butter starts bubbling, add approximately one-third cup of pancake mix to the center of the pan and gently spread it to desired thickness.

11.) Turn down heat to medium-low. When bubbles appear on batter side of hotcake, flip the cake, adding more butter if necessary.

12.) To serve, place apple compote over top of pancake. Combine coconut yogurt with desired about of maple syrup and drizzle over top of cake. Enjoy!

As a child, I would always wonder why my mom would prepare huge containers of homemade kimchi, a huge effort that often took a few days, laborious tasks, and many supplies. From washing huge heads of napa cabbage to meticulously salting each leaf by hand, from making seasoning pastes by hand to submerging each cabbage head in this spicy paste, making kimchi is a massive undertaking and, therefore, in our home, a family experience. Instead of buying family-sized containers at our local Korean market, she would make these jars and then distribute them to her friends at her weekly picnics. Why would she spend so much time, money, labor, and energy to make something she a) could enjoy at a cheaper cost, and b) would give away almost immediately? Why did I have to run out of her car, deliver jars of food to the doorstep of her friends' homes, and ring the doorbell? Although this phenomenon used to confuse me, I later understood when I started cooking for others that food could be a gift. Despite cheaper, more convenient options, creating kimchi at home represented my mother's care for her friends and her willingness to give a meaningful gift of homemade food.

Similar to how canned chicken soup is incomparable to a homemade version, homemade kimchi has a certain quality that makes it far superior to its supermarket counterparts. Maybe it's because my mom's kimchi is customized to perfectly match my family's palate, but homemade kimchi is unlike any other banchan, or side dish.

Mom's Red Kimchi:

Ingredients:

- 3 heads of napa cabbage
- 2 bunches of green onion
- 2 Korean radish (medium-sized)
- 1 large carrot
- 1 bunch of purple mustard leaf
- 1 cup of coarse Korean sea salt

Sauce ingredients:

- 3 tablespoons of sweet (glutinous) rice flour
- 1 cup of water
- 4 tablespoons of fish sauce
- Korean salted shrimp (fermented)
- 2–3 tablespoons of sugar or sugar substitute
- 6 tablespoons of gochugaru
- 2–3 bulbs of garlic
- 1 medium-sized ginger root
- 1 yellow onion

optional:

- bunch of Korean watercress

Steps:

1.) From the head, slice directly down from the top of an upright napa cabbage, head to the middle. After this cut, rip the two slides apart; it should be a clean tear with two even pieces remaining. Do this again with the two remaining pieces so you have quartered the cabbage.

2.) Repeat with other cabbage heads. Rinse and deep clean quartered cabbage leaves, making sure to remove any bugs in-between leaves.

3.) In a large container, pour enough water to soak cabbage. Mix in Korean sea salt (make sure you are using Korean sea salt—iodized sea salt will not work and will make the result extremely bitter) and soak cabbages overnight.

4.) After this soak, cabbage pieces should not be stiff; they should be quite wilted. Remove water and rinse cabbage.

5.) Taste a piece of this cabbage. If it is too salty, rinse again before setting pieces aside.

6.) In a saucepan, add water and rice flour for the sauce (make sure the heat is not on).

7.) Once the mixture has thickened and is bubbling, remove from the heat and let cool, stirring occasionally to reduce clumps.

8.) Julienne carrot, mustard leaves, Korean radish, green onion, and watercress (if using).

9.) Pulse or blend garlic and onion until smooth.

10.) In the cooled rice flour mix, add fish sauce, salted shrimp, sugar, and gochugaru. Mix well until there are no clumps.

11.) Add julienned vegetables and blended garlic, ginger, and onion to the paste.

12.) Get a large, airtight container ready as you massage the thickened sauce/paste onto each leaf of each section of cabbage. Once each leaf and section is well-covered, pack it into the container. Make sure to use all, or as much of the paste as possible.

13.) Once packed into the container, put plastic wrap over the top of the kimchi, pressing down firmly. Optional: wrap and sanitize a heavy object to push the plastic down and put pressure on the kimchi.

14.) Leave in a cool place for one day (if you live in a hot area, a half day is fine).

15.) After this, store in the refrigerator. After a few days, kimchi is ready! The longer it ages, the better it is.

16.) Serve with any Korean dish after cutting into bite-sized pieces! Enjoy!

These stories from my own life prove how food is truly a labor of love and connectivity. Food is, therefore, the currency of love; it is transferrable, and there is something special about sharing or cooking a meal with someone you love.

Familial love is different from any other love because of its inherent intimacy. But love can extend outside of close human relationships; it can also be a level of care someone or something extends to another. Although love is more passionate than care, food can also be a vehicle to express levels of dedication and devotion.

New York University: The Lens of Food

As the fall semester of 2020 began at NYU amidst the coronavirus (COVID-19) pandemic, incoming freshmen moved into school dormitories and apartments, eager to begin the first few days of what would be their undergraduate college career. Due to COVID-19 regulations in New York and NYU's housing system, students were expected to self-quarantine in their accommodations for two weeks, and the school planned to parcel out takeout dining hall meals for its students.

What happened next took social media by storm. TikTok videos of the meals supplied, posted by these freshmen, went viral. Within hours, NYU soon became a laughingstock for its exorbitant tuition prices and less-than-meager housing meals. One video showcased what was labeled a "watermelon chicken salad," another lunchbox revealed a "chicken Caesar salad" with a small bag of tortilla chips and a packet of balsamic vinegar, and one "vegan"-labeled dinner revealed a small steak salad. Given the prestigious image NYU prides itself on, people online were given a real glimpse of what life at NYU currently looked like—cheese, watermelon chunks, and boiled chicken breast. It was only after instant backlash and nationwide coverage of these college-supplied meals flooded social media NYU took steps to rectify its mistakes, issuing students thirty dollars of delivery food credit in lieu of dinner and promising better options for meal boxes. Local alumni and organizations took it upon themselves and pitched in, delivering groceries and snacks to hungry students.

As other universities started to open back up and follow suit in terms of quarantining their students, food options and meals became competitively high quality. Why?

Beyond the obvious reasons of nationwide backlash, universities across America realized seemingly menial services, like dining hall food options, say a lot about campus values. As NYU students shared their meager meals on TikTok, people mocked the apparent greediness of the university. Some questioned the audacity of NYU's exorbitant tuition prices when compared to the meals they supplied for their students. For context, NYU is one of the most expensive schools to attend, with a projected cost estimate nearing eighty thousand dollars. The image NYU portrayed to the world was one of another ruthless, private corporation more concerned about generating profits than truly taking care of and proving for its students. By sending students credit to delivery services, NYU was throwing money at a problem, typic of corporate greed in formulating solutions. On the other hand, when alumni and community organizations engaged in relief efforts, they did so in the form of food, which speaks to human kindness and connection.

In our society, food represents so much more than a basic necessity for survival. Food is a representation of care, which is why NYU, an *educational* institution, damaged its image and suffered so much vitriol due to its supplied food items—or lack thereof.

Rabbit Food

For a large portion of my life, I never considered that veganism or vegetarianism would ever be a part of my particular lifestyle. I loved steak, seafood, cheese, and most other animal products and by-products. In my mind, my favorite foods and a plant-based lifestyle were mutually incompatible.

I still enjoy these protein sources, but I also discovered new protein sources I equally love. Some of my favorite plant-based foods are naturally high in protein, like chickpeas, tofu, beans, and lentils.

When I started to cook for myself, I experimented with a lot of vegetarian dishes. At the time, this was not a choice. Since I was a young, eager "chef," my parents let me express myself through cooking, but this meant I had to eat everything I made, and typically only use leftover ingredients that were already in the refrigerator. Although this was frustrating at the time, these rules shaped two of the perceptions I hold about food.

1.) Animal protein should not go to waste.

2.) Vegetables are delicious! They aren't just a side dish to the main protein source.

Some of my favorite plant-based items are vegan cheese, chickpeas/beans/lentils over ground meats, tofu and cauliflower steak, and vegan protein powder.

Crispy Chickpeas

Ingredients:

- 2 cans of chickpeas
- olive oil
- paprika
- garlic powder
- salt and pepper
- cumin
- lemon

Steps:

1.) Rinse and dry chickpeas (optional: keep liquid if chickpeas are unsalted for an egg substitute for vegan baked goods).

2.) Toss with olive oil and two teaspoons each of paprika, garlic powder, and cumin. Add the juice of half a lemon and bake at 375 degrees Fahrenheit until crispy and crunchy.

3.) Remove from oven and salt to taste.

4.) Serve on top of salad, as a snack, or over soup.

Food says a lot about who we are, where we come from, and what we believe in. For instance, one of my best friends, Anaïs, eats cheese religiously. Whenever we go grocery shopping, she makes sure to pick out a couple of snacking cheeses she can later enjoy with fruit or crackers. One day, as we were talking about our favorite foods from our cultures, she mentioned cheese was emblematic of her French culture. At that moment, I realized even our snacking tendencies reveal so much about ourselves. Food is symbolic. And in the same way Anaïs's love for cheese is in her blood, choosing to engage in food decisions that help the world says a lot about who you are.

When I started outreach for this project, I was approached by Rowan Born; her story about different perspectives on plant-based lifestyles proves how what you eat is inherently an extension of *you*.

One of my favorite snacks, avocado toast, is an easy vegan meal to prepare.

Rowan Born—Redefining My Veganism

"I think there's a lot of thought going into how to deconstruct the word 'normal' to the fact that being vegan is a divergent diet from normal but it's not a substitute for what's normal. It's its own thing."

– ROWAN BORN

The vegan lifestyle has exploded in popularity over the past few years, as people make lifestyle changes to accommodate for the changing world. Veganism, a diet that excludes not only animal products but also animal by-products, has been the subject of much conversation.

You've probably seen non-vegans rolling their eyes after seeing a vegan rendition of one of their favorite foods. Maybe you have shaken your head at the impossibility of cutting out meat from your own diet. There are many reasons why people go vegan. Some care deeply about animal rights and taking down the structures that exploit them for human benefit; others are passionate about the environment and the global repercussions of the meat and dairy industries. Veganism has also been extremely effective for some to mitigate some of the harsh effects of disease and health problems. For Rowan Born, however, her foray into veganism began with an altogether separate reason: the need to restrict.

Since her freshman year of high school, Rowan had engaged with some form of a meatless diet. As an only child, Rowan looked for ways to entertain, educate, and stimulate herself, so she turned to the Internet. Right before she began her first year at her high school in

Pensacola, Florida, she experimented with vegetarianism after watching documentaries like *Forks Over Knives* and learning about how veganism could positively influence health and issues like heart disease and cancer. She also consumed media from not-so-reputable sources, like early vegan and fitness influencers, whose expertise was solely from their personal views and experiences with plant-based diets. At the time, Rowan was young and impressionable, and she struggled with her own issues with body image. A plant-based diet not only sounded like a panacea for her health anxieties, but it also gave her a strict structure she could adhere to and restrict her diet further.

Although it was a struggle for Rowan to maintain and explain a divergent diet in the South, where animal by-products are frequently main courses of meals, she started to become more aware of what she was putting into her body.

For the first time in her life, Rowan's lifestyle was drastically different from those around her. As a white, Christian girl, she had grown up in the South as a part of the larger population majority. In going plant-based, she started to become hyperaware of how unaccommodating people generally were in terms of being different. In her own words,

"Things are just not accommodated for people who have a divergent way of living, and I was beginning to discover that. I was raised, white, in the South, with a Christian family, so I was pretty much in the majority population demographic. And so, going plant-based was the first real immediate experience I had with having to look for something outside of the norm and realizing how that can be a challenge, and how that can

help me empathize and understand other people's challenges they face in a similar accord."

Although her initial motivation stemmed from a place of unhappiness and body image, she found that in researching veganism, a new obsession grew. This time, however, it was a healthy obsession, one with learning more about nutrition and how to solve her existing health problems with digestion. In her sophomore year of high school, Rowan converted to an entirely vegan diet. This time, however, she had the intent of removing products that weakened her digestion system.

As one of two vegans at her high school, she faced a lot of backlash with her diet and was even bullied for it at times, as people harshly gave her their opinions on her diet. Despite this, Rowan found fulfillment in veganism, specifically by choosing what she wanted to put into her body and why. In exploring her plant-based diet, she realized one thing—for her, veganism was no substitute for the foods she had eaten prior to becoming vegan. Instead, it is an entirely new way of living. To put it succinctly, the question should not be, "Does this vegan bacon taste like actual bacon?"—it should be, "Does this vegan bacon taste good?"

Along with discovering different foods and making realizations about her life, Rowan grew her passion for the environment through her diet. What we put out into the world is a direct reflection of who we are, and food is no exception. As she worked through her personal struggles with body image, her reason for being vegan changed. No longer was it a structure to adhere to that would reinforce negative eating behaviors, but it was a tangible way for her to care about the environment through the lens of her diet.

As Rowan celebrates seven years of being vegan, she reflects on her food choices now and describes her vegan lifestyle as something she has normalized to the point she doesn't think too deeply about it. At the same time, she actively tries to destigmatize the vegan lifestyle to her friends, especially when they express curiosity about the diet. For example, although she does not eat meat anymore, she is open to trying new foods in different countries when she travels. In 2019, she studied abroad in Greece, which is not especially known for being a vegan-friendly country. While in Greece, she ate spanakopita, a Grecian dish of cheese and spinach wrapped in filo pastry dough. By focusing on engaging with the food culture in Greece instead of adhering to strict veganism, Rowan shows her dismissal of "all-or-nothing" culture, which espouses the idea vegans are either all in or not at all.

For Rowan, the point of veganism is listening to her body and responding to it with the fuel that will help her feel her best. By doing this, she also is able to fulfill her passion in helping the world through the environment. Although it started from a place of wanting to restrict her diet and feed into her negative visualization of herself, she found solace in bettering her body with the decisions she made for herself. With time, her vegan diet was no longer a projection of insecurity, but a representation of health and intentionality.

"Being vegan, like, healed a lot of [my unhealthy tendencies to overexercise, restrict, and deprive myself]. Although it took years, and to some extent, I still struggle sometimes with being

very picky about what I eat, but overall, there's not this huge guilt complex with it anymore."

What I learned from interviewing Rowan was how misunderstood vegans are. Although they are playfully mocked on social media and misrepresented by extremist vegan "influencers," most vegans operate with the mind-set of mindfulness and intentionality. They are aware of what they put into their body and into the world.

Although some "vegan influencers" are known for their extremist perspectives of their vegan lifestyle, and certain comments on social media cooking channels can sway our perception of vegans, it is important to remember all vegans are different; thus, we should not ascribe negative characteristics to the whole of a community. All the plant-based people I have met in my life have only educated me about their lifestyles and never shamed me for my personal food choices.

Despite its novelty in years past, the vegan lifestyle is becoming more and more accepted across the world, as the need for plant-based substitutes increases with the rate of environmental change. Many even see vegan food as "trendy," and the backlash many early plant-based influencers faced in past years is not as much an issue anymore.

Whether or not a vegan lifestyle is right for you is a personal decision. Everyone's body is so different, thus the changes we make to our diet should reflect the needs of our body, not what the media tells us is right for us.

Morgan Natoli—Discovering Cultural and Contemporary Identity

When Morgan Natoli first became vegan, people around her expressed their doubt and cast judgment, questioning her decision to cut out all meat products. Amongst the usual culprits like, "How are you going to get your protein?" Morgan faced critique from her family members, as they preemptively judged her ability to vegan-ize the cultural dishes she had enjoyed in the past.

Coming from an Italian and Spanish family, Morgan grew up surrounded by two distinct, yet compatible food cultures. At an early age, she would watch as her mom baked family recipes inspired by Italian treats like biscotti, pizzelle, and cannoli. After going vegan, however, Morgan realized she had given up staple ingredients needed to make these treats. Undeterred, Morgan sat down with her mom and asked her questions about the origin of her family's cookies in an effort to understand how they came about. After researching the history of these treats, as well as vegan substitutes, Morgan baked a vegan Pane di Pasqua, a braided, yeast-leavened bread with a colored egg in the center. The braids embedded into this bread represent the Holy Trinity of Christian faith, and the wreath-like shape symbolizes the crown of thorns Jesus wore. Finally, the focal point of the pastry, a colored egg, is a symbol for the birth of Jesus Christ.

Baking a traditionally (and obviously) non-vegan pastry was a big deal. Not only did this accomplishment prove Morgan could still enjoy her favorite foods while nourishing her body in the way she needed to, but it was also a signifier of her broadened cultural awareness. Although critics had told her she would lose her roots by going vegan, Morgan actually learned more about her cultures through her seemingly "restrictive" diet. As she learned to make vegan versions of her favorite foods from scratch, Morgan became more aware of both the quality of foods she was consuming as well as the cultural significance to her.

For Morgan, going vegan helped her feel connected with her heritage. As her skills in the kitchen grew, so did her mindfulness about the world, and how she fit into it.

My favorite store-bought dumplings are these vegan pot stickers from H Mart

Veganism is undoubtedly a huge lifestyle change for someone used to consuming meat. But my journey with plant-based foods and diets has led me to one major conclusion: animal products and plant-based foods should not exist in opposition to each other. Rather, they can complement each other and lay the foundations of conscious consumption.

Fuel

———

If you were going to run a marathon in two hours, what would you eat?

You probably wouldn't go for a Big Mac or a whole pizza, would you?

Because engaging with others through food is so important, it gets very easy to complicate food. One of the signs of disordered eating patterns is thinking too much about food and meals. For some, days revolve around meals or even the restriction of food. But in its simplest form, food is fuel.

In previous chapters, I discussed the art, love, passion, and cultural significance behind food. At its very core, though, food is something organisms consume for the purpose of energy. In order to fuel ourselves and expend energy on tasks that make us who we are, we need to eat. But a lot of complications come with what should be a relatively simple activity. Some question, "How much should I eat?" Others consider how their diet impacts their physical body, whether their purpose is to build muscles and gain body mass, lose weight, or simply to engage in physical activity. This phenomenon can be directly correlated to our generation's ability to connect with others both in person and virtually, as well as the abundance of options we face in this current food contemporary moment, which I will discuss later in future chapters.

So how do we fuel ourselves?

Today, so many rules and regulations exist in the media about food. One example of this is the advent of social media influencing in the fitness sphere. Fitness influencer vlogs, cheat day videos, and calorie-centric programs seem to commonly regard food as a fueling unit, hence the macronutrient calculation, the term "cheat day," and obsessive calorie counting. Though some will evade the potential pitfalls of such a mentality, others can fall prey to it and inadvertently develop a toxic relationship not just with exercise, but also food—both things extremely vital to our life. What we eat says a lot about who we are and what lifestyles we lead, so it makes sense that food can be a huge source of stress for many.

You might already be shaking your head at this, but think about it. What comes to mind if you see someone at a restaurant order a salad? Does this change if they are female-identifying? What about if they are larger or smaller than you?

The point is people are perceptive. Many project this onto themselves, judging their own choices and casting a critical eye at their own lives. As someone who has struggled with multiple eating disorders, I completely relate with the feeling of being at the mercy of food, rather than being the one in control. But to properly fuel ourselves, we have to listen to our bodies. Every body is vastly different; therefore, there is no one "right" way to eat. What you consume should be an answer to the needs of your body.

Morgan Natoli—Listening to Your Body

At age sixteen, Morgan Natoli was diagnosed with Crohn's disease, an inflammatory bowel disease that negatively effects the gastro-intestinal system. After doing research, Morgan decided to try veganism in an attempt to improve some of her painful symptoms, which included bloating and stomach pains.

For Morgan, going vegan was an answer to her digestive concerns.

When we help ourselves and do things that improve our quality of life, it's extremely empowering.

What is interesting about Morgan's story is it is continual. Since our bodies are constantly changing, it is only natural our needs do too. In March 2020, Morgan found herself questioning if veganism was right for her at that point in her life. For many people, March 2020 was an uncertain, confusing time in which huge changes in lifestyles, location, and day-to-day activities were shared experiences. For someone with a divergent diet like Morgan, sourcing food she could eat became harder than usual and, due to her status as someone high-risk for COVID-19, her situation seemed even more bleak. Instead of sticking to the rules she had abided by in years past, she decided to do the very thing that prompted her vegan journey. Once again, Morgan evaluated her needs and listened to what her body was telling her.

I still remember Morgan's excitement when I pledged to go vegan for three weeks and her knowing smiles when I told her it was too hard a few weeks later. When I first started to experiment with plant-based foods and meals, I would always text her first about this development, and she would unfailingly respond with words of encouragement.

For Morgan, a vegan diet was a solution to the problems she faced with her digestive system. But as her lifestyle changed with the circumstances she was in, she changed her diet to answer to her new needs. And that is a perfect example of truly listening to your body. Your body is constantly changing. Even if this means a change on a smaller scale, adaptation is a necessary process of growth and fueling oneself.

When I was interviewing Morgan, I was struck by her definition of "listening to your body." Personally, when I started my own recovery process, I focused more on the physical aspect in terms of changes I made to my life. For me, this meant eating what I considered to be healthy. Ultimately, my journey was derailed, as this mind-set of changing just my physical needs took me down the path of orthorexia, an unrecognized eating disorder where individuals overcomplicate nutrition and calories to the point of obsession. As I considered what went wrong, I came to the conclusion my eating habits didn't just need a physical change—they also needed a mental one. Instead of just focusing on nutritional changes, I should have considered what my mind wanted as well. Although some foods are not as nutritionally dense as others, that shouldn't derail you from enjoying what your body and mind crave. This doesn't mean to indulge in junk food, but to let yourself enjoy what makes your mind and body feel good. Listen to your cravings, because your body is telling you something.

I love cooking for my friends, partly because it is in my nature to love "showing" new things to people, and partly because I never eat my leftovers.

One night in my junior year of college, I invited two of my friends, Elliot and Brandon, over for dinner. Anaïs, my roommate, and I had been hosting weekly *Harry Potter* movie nights and dinners. In the past, we had ordered tacos from Sonoratown in DTLA, and pad see ew, pad thai, drunken noodles, and green curry from Luv2Eat Thai Bistro in Thai Town. As a host, I also cooked dinner and movie snacks frequently, whether that was pasta, oysters, roasted vegetables, nachos, or spicy Korean rice cakes. For this specific night, I decided to prepare one of my favorite dinners, an arugula salad, for the group.

One of the meals we shared together, tacos from Sonoratown in Downtown Los Angeles

Many people eat salads for the convenience factor. Others eat them for their health benefits. When I make a salad, however, it is definitely not convenient. I often juggle using four to five kitchen appliances as I scramble to prepare each ingredient. In my signature salad, I use arugula and quinoa for the base, cast-iron chicken and roasted Japanese sweet potatoes baked in a fermented chili glaze for bulk, cilantro and basil for flavor, and cucumbers, raw beet, and chicken fat croutons for added texture. For dressing, I use a raw cashew dressing inspired by one of my favorite salad joints. Like an orchestra, each ingredient plays a crucial role in this meal.

One of my favorite simple salads of kale, lemon vinaigrette, parmesan cheese, almonds, and dried cranberries

My Signature Salad

One of the main reasons why I tend to use healthy ingredients while cooking is because I strongly believe food should make you feel good. When I cook, I aim to not only fuel my body, but also to recharge my mind. Cooking is a way for me to reconnect with my mind, process or begin a day, and center myself. By cooking what I consider to be healthy, I communicate to my body that I am ready to take on a day.

Ingredients:

Salad Base:

- arugula
- quinoa
- cucumbers
- raw beet
- basil
- cilantro
- Japanese sweet potato
- harissa or fermented Calabrian chili paste (sub. sambal olek)
- honey
- garlic powder or dehydrated garlic
- chicken tenderloins or thighs

Dressing:

- ⅓ cup of cashews
- 3 tablespoons of nutritional yeast
- 2 tablespoons of soy sauce
- juice of one lime
- 4 cloves of garlic
- ⅓ cup of water

- ½ cup of cilantro
- 1 tablespoon of garlic powder
- sriracha to taste
- chili flakes to taste
- salt to taste

Steps:

1.) Wash sweet potato, bake at 375 degrees Fahrenheit for one hour.

2.) Blend or pulse all dressing ingredients and store in refrigerator or cool place.

3.) Cook quinoa and cool.

4.) Chop and peel all vegetables, wash and tear herbs, and assemble raw salad ingredients.

5.) Take out potato and open up the skin as you would a baked potato.

6.) Combine chili paste of choice with garlic powder. Paint on mixture inside the open-faced potato (white flesh).

7.) Drizzle with honey before returning to oven at 425 degrees Fahrenheit, bake for additional fifteen minutes.

8.) Dry chicken tenderloins. You can also marinate chicken in any marinade, but I recommend a brine-y, spicy flavor profile. Ingredients for a pickled jalapeño garlic chicken or mild harissa chicken are below. If you don't pre-marinate, just dry chicken tenderloins with a paper towel, salt and pepper both sides, and add dry seasonings. My choices would be garlic powder, a hint of cumin, thyme, oregano, and chili flakes.

9.) Sear chicken on high heat until done (about five minutes for tenderloins, nine minutes for tenders). Let rest on a cutting board for about the same time. Cube chicken before adding it over top of the salad.

10.) With the oil and fat in pan, turn the heat to low. Break up whatever bread you have on hand after toasting it. Once croutons are nice and crispy, kill the heat.

11.) Add chicken, croutons, and dressing to the assembled salad and mix Optional: grato Parmigiano-Reggiano cheese over top for extra creaminess.

Picked Jalapeño Marinade:

1.) -pickled jalapeño brine

2.) -if brine is not sweet, add honey to taste

3.) -garlic powder

4.) -3 cloves of smashed fresh garlic

5.) -thyme

6.) -2 glugs of olive oil

7.) -oregano

8.) -paprika

(salt when cooking, to taste)

Harissa Chicken:

1.) - harissa paste

2.) - minced garlic
   - optional: light drizzle of honey
   - olive oil

3.) - lemon juice and salt (add when cooking)

PART TWO

THE FOOD REALITY

Eating Through the City: Los Angeles

When thinking of food capitals around the world, a few locations automatically come to my mind. To clarify, I consider food capitals places where I would travel in part to experience the local cuisine. In America, some of the most common include cities like New York, San Francisco, Houston, New Orleans, and Seattle—places where different ethnic groups have historically settled and therefore influenced the city's cuisine.

Greek food from Papa Cristo's* on Pico and its interior grocery store

---

On a global scale, however, this list typically includes countries where cooking is a central part of culture, including Morocco, Italy, France, Brazil, Haiti, Japan, and the Philippines. What is so beautiful about Los Angeles, therefore, is it is a mecca for cultural understanding through taste.

I moved to Los Angeles in 2018 and immediately fell in love with the city. This was the view from my freshman dorm room.

From November 2019 to July 2020, I held the position of a marketing intern for The Wonderful Company, which is headquartered in Santa Monica, California. Before COVID-19, I remember my morning drives to HQ, which took approximately twenty to thirty minutes, depending on traffic. My travel route started with getting on the freeway and merging onto Pico Boulevard. On my drives, I would open my windows, play my favorite songs, and breathe in the cold, crisp air as I prepared myself for a day of work. One landmark I would always count on as a directional cue during these drives was a mural on Pico, which signaled to me that I would turn left on Barrington. The mural depicted a quote from late *Los Angeles Times* food reporter and critic Jonathan Gold. With my history in journalism, specifically critical reviews, and my passion for food, it makes sense Gold has always been someone I looked up to in terms of my career goals. As a journalist, Jonathan Gold put a spotlight on food destinations that were not the typical Michelin-starred restaurants that lie on the high-end spectrum of cooking. Not only did he bring attention to small businesses, but he also was responsible for redefining both LA's food culture and the genre of food critical review.

But his quote that is on the mural is not one I was familiar with, nor is it one of his more popular quotes. Instead, it is a simple phrase, but one whose implications help contextualize the diversity inherent to Los Angeles—

"Pico…where I learned how to eat."

Although this statement may seem simple enough, its implications help contextualize the rich history of Los

Angeles. One of the primary ways we can see this history is through the diverse range of cuisines the city has to offer, usually localized to different neighborhoods, like Koreatown, Little Ethiopia, Chinatown, Little Tokyo, Thai Town, Little Armenia, and Filipinotown.

Beverly Soon Tofu—Social Media and Restaurants

As COVID-19 swept the nation, beginning in early 2020, life as we knew it paused. For some, this time was a much-needed break from life's responsibilities. But for many, the coronavirus upended jobs, leading to financial uncertainty and insecurity for many individuals and families.

One sector that was greatly impacted was the food service and hospitality industry. Specifically, small businesses as well as large franchises had to make changes in terms of their business models, accessibility, and health precautions to survive in their respective markets. For some restaurants, this meant converting their parking lots into outdoor dining patios. Others adapted by offering delivery services through third-party courier services, like Uber Eats, Postmates, and Grubhub. Yet despite some of their best efforts, many restaurants had to face their new reality and close up shop.

One of Los Angeles' most prominent destinations is Koreatown, which is probably most recognized for its cuisine. One of its most beloved institutions, Beverly Soon Tofu, first opened its doors in 1986 before soon tofu jiggae, or silken tofu soup, was really considered a Korean specialty. In opening Beverly Soon Tofu, founder Monica Lee took soondubu, a simple working-class business lunch, to an entirely new level. Experimenting with different flavor combinations, she developed a whole menu for her restaurant that dedicated itself to soondubu jjigae. Eight years later, another entrepreneur, Hee Sook Lee, started a soondubu jjigae restaurant, Duk Chang Dong, or BCD Tofu House, to add to the growing popularity of the soup. Within a few years, BCD scaled up to cities across America and East Asia. Soon, soondubu followed the same pathway of LA Galbi in its return to the motherland, reclamation by South Koreans, and current status of a Korean food staple.

In light of COVID-19, however, Beverly Soon Tofu faced a problem. With Los Angeles' county restrictions for restaurants and outdoor dining/takeout services, the restaurant found itself struggling to stay afloat. As an acclaimed institution by famous chefs, food critics, and regular diners, Beverly Soon Tofu's closure announcement on September 7, 2020, came as a shock to many who had enjoyed their hot soup offerings in the past. As the news took social media by storm, food influencers and news publications picked up the story and promoted it across platforms like Instagram and TikTok. Pretty soon, Beverly Soon Tofu saw lines wrapping around the block, backed-up phone orders, and an overloaded online ordering system, as diners hoped to have one last taste of this historical restaurant. As September 20 approached, lines only grew, with people actually camping out in lines before the restaurant opened on its final days. On its last day of service, which was walk-in only, Beverly Soon Tofu sold out of its menu within hours of opening.

As the coronavirus pandemic shifted (and continues to change) the normalcy of life, the food landscape irrevocably changed. With more closures of some of LA's most iconic eateries, like Dominique Ansel Bakery Los Angeles, Broken Spanish, Ma'am Sir, and Jun Won Restaurant (amongst many others), existing restaurants feel the pressure and stress of surviving in the food service and hospitality industry during such a strenuous and uncertain time.

To continue survival, restauranteurs must come up with new ways to market themselves, which has been primarily done through social media. Large restaurant groups like Chipotle established a strong presence this past year on TikTok, and its marketing team's knowledge of the platform's trends and tools allows for it to only strengthen its brand visibility. However, the same cannot be said for local mom-and-pop shops, some of which are owned by people who are not fluent in social media. This may include second-language English speakers or elderly restaurant owners. To preserve some of our favorite, historically significant institutions, especially in big cities, we should consider how our choices can impact the food landscape. In the same way our choices reflect who we inherently are, our food decisions reflect on the culture we want to promote in the future.

One of my favorite dishes actually has its origins in Los Angeles: LA Galbi. This Korean American dish of marinated, flanken cut short ribs, usually charcoal-grilled, remains a pillar of some of my earliest food memories. I remember how my relatives would look on in fascination and in laughter as I devoured their homemade galbi, licking my small fingers and leaving only clean bones, a faint reminder of what was. My mouth waters every time I think about this tender cut of beef and its delicately sweet yet salty flavor. Now, as a broke college student, LA Galbi is more of a delicacy than anything else, and enjoying it means splurging with my savings or budgeting this takeout order from my monthly grocery spending. No matter how old I grow, however, I will always savor the delicious flavors of LA Galbi.

LA Galbi is representative of Korean immigrants in Los Angeles during the mid to late 1900s, and thus Korean Americans today. Although its origination was unclear up to this point, I had the opportunity to interview Christina Kim, whose grandmother was the first to develop this now iconic dish.

LA Galbi

One of the biggest mysteries of Korean cuisine is the origin of this iconic Korean dish.

This is LA-style galbi, from BCD Tofu House.

I had the chance to speak to Caroline Lee, a Los Angeles native whose family immigrated from South Korea in the early 1970s. For Caroline, Los Angeles isn't just her home—it's also her story. Before she was born, her family was among some of the first Korean immigrants to America. After immigrating to Greensboro, North Carolina, from South Korea, her family soon made local headlines. Despite her mother's limited English skills at the time, she was interviewed by a reporter from *The Greensboro Times* for a story that would eventually headline as "Korean Girl Likes Asian Boys."

After moving to Los Angeles in the early 1970s, Caroline's family settled in the north Hollywood area. Despite this, her family drove all the way to what is now Koreatown, to the sole Korean market in Los Angeles at the time. Located on Olympic Boulevard, the Olympic Market helped first wave Korean immigrants source Korean ingredients to remedy their homesickness through food. Another way early Korean Americans developed communities was through shared Christian faith. Even today, the Korean American church is an experience unique to Korean American Christians. Despite how large these churches can be, unity, togetherness, and closeness are characteristics commonly associated with these edifices. On the flip side, because of the close relations between churchgoers, leadership arguments are also common. At the end of the day, however, most will come to associate the Korean American church with a sense of community, which is often exemplified by communal meals after services.

In 1973, Yun Ok Chun, Caroline's grandmother, visited the Olympic Market to purchase meat to marinate for galbi, which was traditionally made with thick cuts of short rib meat. For many Koreans, galbi is a special occasion food, and Yun Ok had planned on preparing and serving this popular dish for her church's lunch that coming Sunday. That day at the market, Yun Ok had an idea that would come to influence Korean cuisine not only in America, but also in South Korea. Instead of asking the butcher for a traditional galbi cut, she requested a flanken cut, in which slices of short rib cut with a small cross-section of bone would be visible. After questioning this strange request, the butcher rejected her proposal and offered a traditional thick cut. Undeterred, Yun Ok became even more determined to procure this cut and continued to insist upon flanken cut short ribs until the butcher relented.

At the market, Yun Ok had a stroke of genius. Not only was cutting the meat flanken-style beneficial in terms of marinating meat, but it also made galbi convenient to grab by the bone and eat. When Yun Ok served her galbi to the Korean church on Sunday, it was an instant hit. Soon after, butchers were getting more and more requests to sell short ribs flanken-style. Before long, flanken-style short ribs became an option at most Korean butchers, and shortly after, pre-marinated, flanken-cut galbi become a popular item at the Olympic Market.

Pretty soon, this trend cemented itself in the hall of fame of Korean cuisine, as the cut and marination style of cooking came back to South Korea, where locals could find it at their local market or restaurant. South Koreans coined it "LA Galbi," based on the one description they knew for sure: it was from Los Angeles.

One reason this story resonates so deeply with me is because, as funny as it may sound, I relate with LA Galbi. Not only was this dish my favorite food growing up, the journey of this dish from its origins in southern California to its reclamation in South Korea parallels my personal cultural understanding. I think the concept of feeling "reclaimed" by one's heritage culture is a familiar journey to many Korean Americans and speaks to the Korean community's strength globally.

I think the first time I realized how special Koreatown in Los Angeles is was when my relatives from South Korea visited. After their arrival, they mentioned how they were looking forward to specific restaurants to try in Koreatown. After registering my initial shock, I wondered why they specifically looked forward to trying Korean food in America. Upon their departure, one of my relatives remarked how he would miss the Korean food in Los Angeles. My confusion only deepened upon hearing this, and I asked him to explain. For him, Korean food in America is different because of the inexpensive availability of ingredients like meat and certain vegetables, which bolsters traditional Korean dishes. What became clear to me at that moment was how Koreatown is not a meager replication of South Korean neighborhoods; rather, it is a destination in and of itself that offers so much to the ongoing story of Korean culture.

Korean barbeque from Gil Mok, a.k.a. The Corner Place

On the flip side, Los Angeles is also home to fads and trends in the food world, some more appealing than others. Some lambast LA's seemingly ridiculously priced avocado toasts, pressed juices, and celebrity gyms. But in the same way LA hosts diverse foods, it also is home to one of the nation's widest income disparities. In less than five minutes, one can drive from a Michelin-starred fine dining restaurant to a local taco stand selling tacos for a dollar.

Misconceptions of Los Angeles as a hub for hopeful social media influencers, expensive food trends, and glamorous lifestyles frame LA's culture as more materialistic and superficial than it actually is. With a median annual income of approximately sixty-five thousand dollars in 2018 according to the US Census Bureau, most LA residents can't afford that fifteen-dollar avocado toast or three-thousand-dollar annual gym pass.[11] In fact, some can only afford fast food. In fact, according to the Los Angeles Food Policy Council, LA has the highest number of people facing food insecurity in the entire nation. Thus, to truly understand LA's food scene, it is imperative to understand all the groups of people who live in its neighborhoods.

Why?

Because food in America is representative of systemic inequality. So, let's talk about food justice.

---

11 U.S. Department of Commerce, Bureau of the Census, *QuickFacts: Los Angeles County, California, 2020* (Ann Arbor, MI, 2020).

Kimchi Soondubu

Ingredients:

- kimchi
- one tube or container of soft tofu (silken)
- single serving of protein of choice
- water, or broth of choice (anchovy is most traditional)
- sesame oil
- soy sauce
- 1–2 stew veggies of choice (I like white/Yukon gold potato and enoki mushrooms)
- gochugaru (Korean red pepper flakes)

Optional:

- green onion
- cheese

Steps:

1.) Chop about one-third cup of kimchi and add it to a small soup pot with its juices. Add protein of choice, gochugaru (to your level of spiciness), one tablespoon sesame oil, and soy sauce to taste.

2.) Stir-fry these ingredients on medium heat together until fragrant, and add one cup of anchovy broth, broth of choice, or water to the soup pan.

3.) Cover and let simmer together on medium-low heat. Once boiling for two minutes, add packet of silken tofu and veggies of choice. Gently stir so the tofu breaks apart in large chunks.

4.) Cover again and turn heat to medium. Once all ingredients have been boiling together and veggies are softened, crack an egg into the boiling water. Kill heat after gently stirring to ensure egg will be evenly poached in the broth. Be careful not to burst the yolk.

5.) Add mozzarella cheese and/or sliced green onions on top if you'd like.

6.) Serve in the pot, with a side of rice.

Note: This dish can be easily made plant-based by removing the initial protein, substituting vegan kimchi, using vegetable broth, and omitting egg at the end. Feel free to experiment with this recipe—it is highly malleable and easy to customize.

Note 2: Cheese is not traditional on this dish, but add whatever tastes good to you!

Food Equality and Justice

——

As a resident of Los Angeles County, I could not write about food without writing about food justice. As Los Angeles' cityscape has changed over the past few decades, so has its food scene. On one hand, this means a greater diversity of food options and cultural appreciation through food cultures. On the other hand, the development of Los Angeles is a huge contributor to gentrification and the occurrences of food deserts.

What is food justice?

Food justice is ensuring healthy, affordable food options are a human right, according to Foodprint.org, a GRACE Communications Foundation project.[12] The basis of this concept is that because food justice has not been achieved, people should take a closer look at the structures and systems in place that prevent it from happening. When we talk about food justice, we have to talk about the racial undertones present in our current food systems. For instance, fast food companies focus

———

12   FoodPrint. "Food Justice," *FoodPrint*, accessed November 13, 2020.

on producing cheap, nutritionally deficient, high-calorie foods, which can leave their patrons feeling sluggish or sick. Instead of focusing on helping those who reside in food deserts, the huge corporations behind some of America's most well-known chains only care about profits, regardless of how they are generated. But what does this have to do with race? Well, low-income people of color in America are disproportionally impacted by the toll of fast food. Food insecurity is a real thing for these people, and more often than not, convenience over health is the obvious choice. Though systems like Cal Fresh/ food stamps and other forms of government relief exist, they are oftentimes inadequate, and the process to qualify for these is long and complicated. Rather than judge this decision, we must look at the fast food industry, which profits off of some of our nation's most vulnerable to perpetuate a capitalist system that generates billions of dollars in revenue.

Let's face a real issue in the food world. It's easy for me to say things like "take food seriously" or "think about adding value to your meals over convenience," but not everyone can or has the means to actually do so. In Part One, I talked about the beauty of food and how we, as humans can form meaningful connections with ourselves, our cultural identities, other cultures, family, and friends through food and cooking. But this stance, and therefore this book, is one that drips with privilege.

Food should be a natural right, but unfortunately, it is not. Although the relationships we make with food and with others are incredible, not everyone has the chance to really think that deeply about food. To some, food is just a unit of energy and therefore survival, not a performance, cultural signifier, creative outlet, or symbolic representation of people. Therefore, although I still stand by everything I have stated in Part One, it is *absolutely vital* to accept not everyone has the ability to enjoy food and really consider its implications.

After being raised in the bubble of Irvine, California, moving to South Central Los Angeles was a shock to the system. To this day, I still practice unlearning some of the "normal behaviors" I had practiced in Irvine, like leaving valuables in cars and walking around at night alone. Although moving to the city from a highly sheltered residential area could seem like a huge shift in my lifestyle, I came to understand many similarities with my home neighborhood and my current one. As a USC student, I am a guest to the community already established in South Central, so I must treat it as such. While I enjoy the privileges of the quality education I receive and the safety provided by my school, I have educated myself on real urban issues of gentrification, transportation, and housing insecurity facilitated by displacement. Although I will never fully be able to understand some of these issues on a firsthand basis, I hope to continue educating myself and taking viable steps to counteract the toxicity unlearned privilege presents.

One of the views from Jeffrey Trail in Irvine, California. The bubble of Irvine can be seen in through its seemingly perfect exterior.

In reaction to these realizations, I took active steps to overcome the task of unlearning my ingrained behaviors to recognize local restaurants and food businesses that contribute to their communities. Specifically, instead of viewing taco stands as a quick, inexpensive bite, I started viewing them for what they really were: small, family-owned businesses that reveal a lot about different food regions in Latin and Central America. Instead of contributing to businesses that could not exist without gentrification, I looked for small businesses to support around me in my direct community of South Central, which is a food desert. For me, this was a way to overcome my internal struggle with coming to terms with my own privilege and figuring out what I could do next.

One of the professors who has had a profound impact on the way I understand American systems and society is Dr. Michael Petitti, who taught one of my favorite classes at USC, CORE 112: American Trash: A Journey Through the Profane, the Popular, and the Profound of America's Cultural Dustbin. In this course, we analyzed different texts from American history, including films like *Pink Flamingos, Taxi Driver, The Birth of a Nation,* and *Fifty Shades of Grey*, as well as literature like *A Rose for Emily, The Sellout, Fear of Flying,* and *Carrie.* One thing these texts had in common was their labeling by someone, be that society or the author, of "trash," "camp," or "kitsch." Through these works, I was able to more deeply understand the undertones of American art culture, and the distinction and blurring of "high-brow" and "low-brow" art in American history.

Dr. Petitti also teaches a Maymester, or USC summer course, in the same interdisciplinary honors program, titled CORE 301: From Pueblo to Postmates: Food and Class in Los Angeles. In this course, Dr. Petitti similarly teaches students about a topic using the lens of another artifact. In this case, however, students analyze their new home of Los Angeles through the lens of food. From eating tours to speaker events, Dr. Petitti aims for students to learn through immersive experiences that leave a lasting impression. With this, he pushes students to analyze how what they eat has a larger, more historically significant meaning on entire communities. Some course objectives include "investigating the complicated intersections of food and class," "exploring the economic effects of morphing into an international food city by examining Los Angeles' diverse population, and issues of immigration, homelessness, capitalism, and globalism," and "considering financial benefits, consequences, and setbacks of food production and consumption within a city widely considered at the cutting edge of America's obsessive food culture."

In CORE 301, students are expected to engage with the food community in Los Angeles by interviewing individuals across the city each week and posting to their respective class's Tumblr site. In 2020, the class shifted to virtual interviews whereas in past years, these interviews entailed in-person interactions with historically significant sites and people. To Dr. Petitti, historical and cultural class struggles can be seen through food signifiers across the city, which are often "hidden in plain sight." Just like the food scene in LA, CORE 301 shifts to accommodate changes each year the course has been offered. For instance, in 2018, also the first year of CORE 301, Dr. Petitti noticed most students considered themselves to be "foodies," or what he describes as "people who are in-touch with what is happening in the food world." In 2019, however, he noticed a shift in his students, who seemed to emphasize their interest in LA's history despite whether or not they had an interest in food. Most recently, in 2020, as students and professors adjusted to a new online format of classes due to a global pandemic, the course experienced dramatic shifts in activities, assignments, and hands-on experiences that were typic of the prior two years. Despite all the differences within the three years of CORE 301, one thing remains constant: students' vested interests in issues of gentrification. Given the frameworks of the class, with emphases on food and class, it should be no surprise students living in the general South Central area are aware of the class divides perpetuated by gentrification, as they themselves inadvertently enter into the system by attending USC.

Although the negative impacts of gentrification in Los Angeles, such as evictions of POC-owned businesses and homes, have been glossed over under the umbrella term of "progress," some initiatives around the city seek to rectify this foregone harm.

First, Defend Boyle Heights is "a revolutionary mass organization committed to fighting gentrification," as described by its social media sites. In East Los Angeles, the five-year-old organization has initiated eviction defense efforts and social media campaigns to raise awareness of the realities of what evictions mean for displaced peoples in Boyle Heights. Everytable is a fast-casual chain that also serves subscription meal plans. With its focus on nutritious and clean ingredients, Everytable abides by its mission to "transform the food system to make delicious, nutritious food accessible to everyone, everywhere." With its pricing model that reflects this mission, Everytable offers a typical meal at only fifty cents more than it costs to produce in underserved areas. To sustain these prices, it offers these same meals in affluent neighborhoods at higher prices, to offset other costs by pricing accordingly. One of my personal favorite initiatives is the Los Angeles Community Fridges, which is an organization primarily active on social media, specifically Instagram, to face the problem of food insecurity and food deserts in Los Angeles. This organization partners with various local businesses to establish community refrigerators that community members can contribute to and take from.

Although these efforts may seem small in terms of the scale of gentrification and cultural erasures Los Angeles has a history of, the mere act of volunteering or supplementing one's community is the first step in counteracting systemic food injustice. Some may argue individuals do not have the power to make a difference, and corporations have the responsibility of reversing the negative impacts of the damage they have wreaked. Though this statement is partially true, it should not be a deterrent for those wanting to take tangible action in their communities, because one person can definitely make a change.

Therefore, donate to a community fridge near you, if you live in a large city. Make your own initiative in whatever community you reside in, whether that means in suburban, urban, or rural areas. Change begins with recognizing a problem, which in this case is food insecurity and deserts.

The Time To Throw Out the Melting Pot

———

Have you ever heard of the metaphor of America as a "melting pot?" The connotation most people have toward this phrase is generally positive, and the portrayal of America as this melting pot has an interesting history that is intertwined with the waves of immigration that took place in America.

"I think food offers a way to connect not only to my family and friends, but also to my heritage. I learned a lot about how the conditions are in which my parents grew up; they saw the food and they like to cook. And it's really interesting to hear their stories about their own personal connections with those dishes, and how they can subscribe to my own personal experiences."

– AUDREA HUANG

Audrea Huang—Taking Cultural Cooking for Granted

When Audrea Huang moved across the country to start her undergraduate career at Wellesley College, it was the first time in her life she experienced homesickness. For her, this homesickness manifested itself in one major way—food.

Growing up, Audrea was not always passionate about her family's traditional Chinese and Taiwanese dishes. In elementary, she was hesitant to bring these home-made dishes to school for lunch based on a fear she would appear to be "too ethnic." Instead, she asked her parents to pack her corn dogs and Wonder Bread sandwiches instead of what she truly craved, 醬爆蛋, or "jiang bao dan," a Chinese egg dish. What is interesting about this story is how common it is for immigrants or children of immigrants in America to feel an automatic shame about their culture or heritage, whether that manifests itself through food or something else. The unconventional look of these foods, or smell of them, signified otherness—and not in a unique, positive way. To quote Audrea directly, "A lot of kids, I think, are hesitant to share their culture with other people, because it's so different. I think it's really wonderful that, like, we can celebrate these differences and learn about different cultures through food."

Some of the dishes I used to be embarrassed to take to elementary school, like japchae, a sweet potato noodle dish with a strong sesame scent

I, for one, have felt the exact way Audrea did when I was in elementary school, hiding my Korean kimbap, dumplings, or kimchi rice. Fast-forward to today, I see people of all races enjoying not only Korean food, but also Korean historical and popular culture and traditions. The ingrained mentality that other food cultures are inferior to that of American, or Western, ones is not uncommon for many immigrants, or children of. This phenomenon is exacerbated by the often-strong scents from various spices or ingredients that accompany most foods from different countries. The more "different" elements a food item were equated to how negatively it was perceived to be. Growing up in a city with a large Asian population helped but did not make me immune to the scrunched-up noses, judgmental expressions, and whispers I had come to expect at lunchtime.

In the current contemporary moment, cultural awareness and celebration is more commonplace than ever. Most big cities offer huge ranges of cuisines, and social media has been instrumental in giving voices to different cultures. Food is a relatively simple way to appreciate another culture, so food negativity in terms of culture and ethnicity is not so much a thing now as it used to be. Although it is easy to support the trending Chinese restaurant or Indian dish, we as consumers should not cast a blind eye to the struggles the people represented in foods have historically faced.

Cultural shame is not uncommon for many children of color growing up in the United States. We see it in the media, we see it in our advertisements, we see it in Hollywood, and we see it in ourselves. For a country that is so diverse, we should be surprised there is still an ideal of "whiteness" we are programmed to compare ourselves to. So, for POC, the experience of growing up in America (thus far) often goes hand-in-hand with the internalization of cultural dilution.

As I tried to verbalize what it meant for me to grow up in America, struggling with my own cultural identity, no phrase really came to mind. As I considered what emotions I felt and reactions I had to different circumstances, one word immediately came to mind—dilution. Therefore, I have coined the phrase **Cultural Dilution** to make sense of my, and many others', experiences.

What is cultural dilution?

Cultural dilution refers to the watering down of cultural elements to make them more "palatable" for the homogenous public, specifically seen in America. Examples of this include the accepted ideals of straight, unassuming hairstyles for women as "professional," and the picking and choosing of cultural items to borrow and, in some cases, appropriate.

The process of dilution goes hand-in-hand with cultural erosion, which is the chipping away at culturally significant traditions and processes in an attempt to "explain" them to the general masses—typically a mass they don't find themselves truly a part of.

This is not to say cultures should not celebrate differences and learn from each other; actually, it means the opposite.

From my personal experience, I often have to unlearn the behaviors that have been so ingrained into me. For instance, when I describe some Korean dishes to my non-Korean friends, I often provide a frame of reference to normalize this food. One example is how I would describe Korean dishes as "Korean 'x,' or a Korean version of 'x.'" To make the best impression of a Korean dish, I feel the need to give a comparison to a dish that is commonly eaten in America. This is cultural dilution, because instead of me telling someone "dwenjang jjigae" is a hearty, fermented bean paste soup, I would simply compare it to American chili. The only commonality between the two is both typically utilize beans as a base, but beyond that, they bear no similarities. The tendency of people who identify strongly with more than one culture is to "dumb" down or simplify traditions to make them "palatable," which leads to the direct eroding of a given culture to those outside of it.

In the same way people who belong to a culture and identify with it have a certain responsibility to accurately portray it to their friends, those outside of that given culture have a similar responsibility to understand why portrayal is so important in this day and age.

What comes to mind when you think about "American" food? Do you think hamburgers and hot dogs? Maybe you think of sandwiches on white bread. Or maybe you simply think of the proliferation of fast food and the glimmering of the golden arches. When I think about American food culture, one word comes to mind—convenience.

In so many parts of the world, food and cooking are sacred traditions, and a heavy emphasis on cooking as a quasi-ritual is common. In America, the concept of experiencing food and dining traditions are experiences catered to the select few. The disconnect between what we eat and its preparation is therefore a very real thing. Think of processed proteins like bacon and deli meats, sugary drinks, and coffees. In a typical American supermarket, we see rows and rows of raw meats—a dissonance from their origins. As diverse as the culinary scene in America is, a trend exists that cannot be totally ignored—the adulteration of sacred traditions and cooking cultures through their American adaptations.

US Immigration Timeline[13] [14] [15]

20–30,000 years ago:

- The first peoples come to America via "Beringia," or the Bering Strait. Thus, the first people to live in what we know as America are immigrants.

1600:

- In the early part of the seventeenth century, European immigrants settle along the Eastern coast for reasons of religious and political freedom, along with the incentive of greater economic opportunity. This immigration population includes Europeans from England (to New England, Virginia), Spain (to Florida), the Netherlands (to New York), and Sweden (to Delaware).

13 "Timeline of Immigration the United States," Internet & Technology, San Diego Government, updated January 2021.

14 U.S. Immigration Timeline," Internet & Technology, History, updated September 3, 2019.

15 "Immigration and Relocation in U.S. History," Internet & Technology, Library of Congress, updated 2021.

- Enslaved Africans also come to America during this time, forcibly enslaved by these early immigrants from their homes in West Africa.

- In 1620, the Pilgrims arrive in Plymouth, Massachusetts. By the early- to mid-century, approximately twenty thousand Puritans have immigrated to this region.

1790:

- The Naturalization Act of 1790 is passed in March; any free white person of "good character" who has lived in the United States for a minimum of two years can now apply for citizenship.

- The first US Census occurs this year in August. The English make up the largest ethnic minority, and one in five Americans are of African descent.

1815:

- A wave of immigration begins from Western and Northern Europe, primarily from Ireland and Germany, three years after the War of 1812, which results in peace between the United States and England. The primary grounds for this wave are rooted in the possibility of economic stability in terms of work opportunities.

- After the Irish Potato Famine of the mid-nineteenth century, immigration from Ireland reaches an all-time high, and by the 1840s, about half of immigrants are from Ireland.

- German and Scandinavian immigrants come to the US for reasons of escaping their home country's problems of unstimulated economy, corruption in politics, and failure in agriculture.

1849:

- In response to the large numbers of poor German and Irish-Catholic immigrants who crowded cities, the "Know-Nothing Party" is created. This political affiliation, with beliefs rooted in white supremacy, made their opposition toward immigration and Catholicism obvious; the formation of this party makes a clear power and class distinction between minorities and majorities in America.

- The California Gold Rush of 1849 prompts approximately twenty-five thousand Chinese immigrants to settle in the Western United States.

1870:

- After the Civil War, a period of economic downturn defines the country, and jobs previously held by immigrants, such as Chinese immigrants in the west, become highly coveted. As competition grows stronger for jobs, anti-immigration sentiment takes hold of the nation.

- Though they represent a minuscule portion of the population, the Chinese face discrimination in the form of riots, strikes, and mob violence.

1880:

- The third and largest wave of American immigration begins, with immigrants coming from different areas, including Southern, Eastern, and Central Europe. This wave of immigration is known for its distribution of approximately four million Italians and two million Jewish people—two ethnic enclaves largely unknown to America at the time.

1882:

- The Chinese Exclusion Act bans Chinese immigrants in search of work from coming to America. Since the Chinese are willing to work more cheaply than job standards at the time, Californians blame the Chinese for the decline in wages.

1890:

- Ellis Island in the New York Harbor is designated as a national immigration port.

1894:

- The Immigration Restriction League is formed with the purpose of targeting immigrants with a law that makes English literacy required for entry into America.

1907:

- The US signs the Gentlemen's Agreement with Japan, which limits Japanese immigration to businessmen and professionals.

1914:

- World War I begins, and immigration slows down. At the same time, xenophobia increases and materializes in the form of persecution, lynchings, and anti-immigrant fears sweeping the nation.

1920:

- After the Ku Klux Klan was revived in 1915, it reaches its peak membership count, and over four million people are now subscribed to the organization. The second iteration of this group not only continues its original stance being anti-Black, but also makes clear its hostilities toward the new wave of immigrants (those who arrived in 1880).

1924:

- The Immigration Quota Act, which was fueled by anti-immigration sentiment, caps the number of immigrants per year at 350,000 and sets National Origins Quotas to limit the numbers of immigrants who come from different countries. By 1929, the act has been edited to exclude 200,000 immigrants from the original cap. The National Origins Quota was used as a tool to control the racial and ethnic makeup of the nation, as quotas set for Southern and Eastern Europeans were far lower than countries seen as more "desirable," like Britain. While quotas were not set for Canada and Mexico, Asians were banned from immigrating.

1952:

- The McCarran-Walter Act officially ends the banning of Asian immigrants to the US.

1965:

- The Immigration and Nationality Act is passed, which eradicates past quotas based on nationality in an attempt to achieve the ideal of a "homogenous US."

1970:

- Immigration from parts of Asia, predominantly from war-stricken countries like Vietnam and Cambodia, surges to over four times their previous numbers.

1980:

- A general policy to admit refugees based on the United Nation's definition is implemented through the Refugee Act.

- In the Mariel boatlift, over one hundred thousand Cuban refugees sail across the sea to Florida in attempts to seek political asylum.

1986:

- The Simpson-Mazzoli Act grants amnesty to over three million previously illegal immigrants.

2001:

- The Development, Relief, and Education of Alien Minors, or "DREAM," grants eligibility for "Dreamers," or undocumented immigrants brought to the US by their parents illegally as children to eventually achieve legal status; the bill does not pass.

2002:

- The Homeland Security Act centralizes the powers of the US Immigration and Naturalization to the newly instituted Department of Homeland Security after the events of 9/11/2001.

2012:

- DACA, or the Deferred Action for Childhood Arrivals, allows some Dreamers to gain protections against deportation.

2017:

- Two executive orders, called "Protecting the Nation from Foreign Terrorist Entry into the United States," are passed. These orders limited US entry from predominantly Muslim countries like Iraq, Syria, Sudan, Iran, Somalia, Libya, and Yemen, as well as North Korea and Venezuela. These orders were infamously known as the "Muslim Travel Ban."

Now that we've gone through a pretty comprehensive history of immigration in what we recognize today as the United States of America, we can make sense of the structures in place that perpetuate modern-day struggles. We can also understand the context of some of America's food capitals and the foods we come to associate with them.

Think of foods you identify with cities, starting with New York. You probably think of pizza, hot dogs, halal carts, and deli meats like Irish corned beef or Jewish pastrami. How about Miami? Maybe you think about the arepas, Cubano sandwiches, empanadas, and tostones. Let's talk about the Cajun and Creole dishes in New Orleans, or the superb Mexican tacos in San Diego. You might even be thinking about the Taiwanese noodles in the San Gabriel Valley, or the delicious KBBQ and flavorful soups found in Koreatown in Los Angeles. Vietnamese pho and bùn are practically synonymous with Westminster and Garden Grove, as are Chinese dumplings and fried rice with San Francisco.

One food trend people love to hate is "fusion" foods. Whether their reasoning is based on theories of cultural appropriation or simply culinary prowess, fusion food is a polarizing subject for foodies. Personally, I think when fusion foods are done tastefully (pun intended), the food cultures represented can be given larger platforms. In addition, it's a good way to introduce a new food culture to someone's palate.

In our current food economy, we don't always consider the origins of some of our favorite dishes. Today, these dishes represent distant memories of the immigrants who came before us and the turmoil they faced. In the same way the violence, discrimination, and racism they faced have been reduced to tone-deaf stories in standardized history textbooks, the diverse cuisines we have the liberty to enjoy have been adapted to quite literally match the American palate. Inherently, this does not have to necessarily be a bad thing. In fact, some of my favorite dishes are actually Americanized versions of their original counterparts.

The danger, however, comes when we associate Americanized foods with an entire culture or ethnicity. In America, there is such a strong history of marginalizing those perceived to be different. Whether discrimination stemmed from race, ethnicity, sexual orientation, or gender, marginalized people have already felt the impacts of mainstream media defining them and telling their stories. When people associate Panda Express with

China, they not only disrespect Chinese food, which is starkly different, but they also disregard the struggles of immigrant America. As people, we should not cast the perspective of colonizers in defining our understanding of culture.

Yes, some people do not live in urban areas and therefore do not have access to diverse food options. Does that mean their food choices are close-minded and therefore discriminatory? *No.* What people can do to reverse the negative impacts of cultural dilution is enrich themselves with information. For some, this may look like relabeling foods as Americanized versions of the original; for others, this could be traveling to a new country to try their national dish. Oftentimes, food transcends language. When I traveled to Seville, Spain, with my family two winters ago, we visited a local breakfast spot. Although we were the only non-locals in the restaurant, we were immediately served a huge meal of Tortilla Española, churros and chocolate, tostadas with olive oil, jamon, cheese, and tomato, and cups of espresso.

My mom and me in Sevilla, enjoying a late breakfast of traditional morning foods like tostadas, chocolate, churros, and cappuccino

Food is something that connects us, but we cannot ignore the cultural implications some foods have in America. Given its background and American's historical attitude toward immigrants, it is critical to understand food in a bigger context that has underlying themes of dilution and erasure. Food is important because it creates an identity—our role is to understand what that identity *is*.

Social Media and Food

In August 2019, I started documenting my home-cooked meals on Instagram. My account, @mendameals, was meant initially for unhealthy documentation purposes—food journaling and tracking calories for personal referencing use. My content was for me, by me. Because I never expected others to see my posts, I captioned my food posts with the calculated calorie totals of the photo in question. However, without marketing my account at all, I noticed friends and family began following this account and commenting positive, uplifting messages on my posts, unaware these snapshots never revealed the larger picture of my mind and intentions. Although the account was started for my personal use, I realized people started following my account, unprompted, because they were interested in my cooking. From family members to mutual friends I hadn't spoken to in years, @mendameals slowly grew without any marketing.

I started concentrating more on the quality of my posts and started interacting more with users who commented on my pictures. Watching people from my present and past follow me gave me a new motivation to cook. I became more adventurous, testing different recipes in an effort to provide fun content for my viewers and tasty meals for myself. I was no longer cooking to lose weight or change my body in a drastic manner; rather, sharing my cooking on social media gave me back the original passion I had for food. As the account grew, I looked into food photography and editing apps in order to make my photos look more appealing and adventured with different cuisines and cooking techniques. I researched plating techniques and tried to make my home-cooked creations as beautiful and appetizing as possible.

Soon, people I didn't even know, or had hardly spoken with in person, started following me. Interacting with others who shared my love for cooking or simply consider themselves "foodies" changed the way I viewed social media. Prior to @mendameals, I had considered social media, specifically Instagram, a toxic environment for me, as I recall feeling out of place in a virtual sphere that emphasized the superficial nature of things. My insecurities with superficial characteristics, like my body and face, led me to disengage with the platform for months at a time, so posting was rare for me. Even when I was with my friends, I hated having my picture taken, afraid my ugliness or fatness would be immortalized. On top of that, with my extremely diverse taste and eclectic style, I struggled to feel truly natural and genuine on my social media profile, where the main subject matter was me.

The account @mendameals was different. Whereas posting on my main account had previously only brought me stress and anxiety, I was actually excited to plate and post photos of my food creations. For me, cooking represents a side of myself I am most proud to share with others—a side that portrays my creativity naturally, instead of content that feels forced. My rare posts on my main Instagram account typically only presented photos of me, photos that showed a beautiful landscape, or a fashionable outfit. I realized now I always have curated my personal content for the purpose of representing the best, most interesting, fun sides of myself, but with @ mendameals, it's easy.

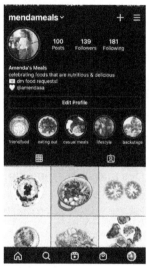

A screenshot of @mendameals

As I previously mentioned, the early days of @mendameals included posts from one of my darkest periods. Upon close inspection, it is pretty clear to see how @ mendameals offers a raw glimpse into my mental headspace. For instance, my inactivity during the late fall and winter of 2019 reflects my mental headspace that was shrouded in anxiety, which resulted in a disengagement from posting on social media platforms. The resurgence of posts in January to March not only shows my return to cooking as a creative outlet, but also my obsession with what I considered "healthy eating." When quarantine started in March 2020, my creations become much more adventurous and my posts more curated, as I used the time at home to experiment and challenge myself. During this time period, I baked and cooked things I had never attempted before: focaccia bread, homemade chocolate chip cookies, pasta al limone, Hawaiian garlic shrimp, and Japanese soba noodle. At the start of @mendameals, carbohydrates—bread specifically—had been one of my fear foods, and I recall being the only apartment mate who would never buy loaves from the grocery store. Developing these recipes not only challenged my cooking abilities, but it also helped me start breaking the food rules I had created and ingrained in my mind. My rules emphasized calories and nutrition—an incomplete picture of what food is.

Focaccia in stages, from prebake to plating, that I baked this summer during quarantine

Although social media helped my relationship with food positively, existing as a creator in the food space is definitely a two-way street. Whereas my followers appreciate my photos and recipes, I feel challenged by them to create delicious meals that reflect my tagline, "celebrating food that is nutritious and delicious." Just like how my posts reflected my varied mental and emotional state, my tagline, or bio, has shifted as I educate myself more about what health and nutrition really mean. My first bio, "cooking meals for a health-conscious college student on a budget," changed as I came to terms with the concept that health looks different for everyone, and my lifestyle was definitely not healthy in the context of my life. As quarantine began in March 2020, I changed my bio to "cooking unhealthy and healthy meals since August 2019."

Although I did have the right idea, I still did not truly understand health. You see, my categorization of foods as unhealthy or healthy overcomplicated food and reinforced past food rules I thought I had outgrown. Health is diverse, and it is highly subjective. Therefore, I changed my tagline for the last time, to emphasize nutrition in the form of clean and nutrient-packed ingredients that benefit one's physical nutrition and satisfy taste buds. Now, "nutritious and delicious" food does not simply mean food that will fuel your body in a physical sense, but also food that stimulates the soul.

One recipe I am most proud of is my Sunday Sauce. When I think of the very moment I started to take cooking seriously, this decadent tomato braised short rib sauce immediately comes to mind. Early one morning, at approximately 2:00 a.m., I returned home from my school's twenty-four-hour library after a particularly long study session. I was stressed, tired, but more than anything, I was hungry. When I got home, I opened my refrigerator to find...nothing. Well, nothing ready to eat. In the busy chaos of the week, I had not gone grocery shopping, and I only had random vegetables and herbs lying around from last week. After looking in the freezer, I found a Ziploc bag of frozen short ribs for a food project I had been planning to tinker with for my food Instagram. I immediately started to defrost the beef and decided to listen to my hunger cues for once—I was going to slow cook six short ribs at 2:00 a.m. in the morning. Why?

Ingredients for the Sunday Sauce

My initial plan was to braise these short ribs in a red wine sauce—a traditional short rib recipe most people probably think of when visualizing short ribs. Given the random ingredients I had, I decided to slow cook my ribs in the extra cans of tomatoes, veggies, leftover pasta sauce, and beef broth I had on hand. After my meat defrosted, I began the time-consuming process of searing and slowly cooking the ribs.

At about 5:00 a.m., the short ribs were ready, and I was waiting for the bread I had put in the toaster to pop out. I was sitting on our living room couch catching up with assignments and planning my work schedule when I heard my apartment mate's room door squeak open. My head shot up, worried I had woken up someone with the noises of my cooking. I watched as my friend Anaïs hobbled to the bathroom and back, looking at me with confused, squinty eyes. "What are you doing?" she asked me. "Oh, I'm just waiting for my short ribs to be ready," I replied, before realizing how strange that would sound to anyone at 5:00 a.m., but especially to someone who had just woken from their slumber. "Well, it smells good," she responded to me.

Soon enough, she was with me in the kitchen, tasting the first bites of my rich tomato sauce with crusty sourdough bread. We sat in silence, blissfully enjoying the perfect marriage of the tangy, crunchy sourdough with the luscious, tender short ribs that had fallen apart in the tomato sauce. Even today, Anaïs always references that perfect sauce, and although I have made it for us again, it will never compare to that quiet morning in our small kitchen.

A photo of the first iteration of this Ragù recipe.

Different ways to serve Sunday Sauce

Early Morning Ragù/Sunday Sauce

Ingredients:

- 1–2 shallots
- ½ bulb of garlic
- 1 large carrot
- olive oil, ghee, or avocado oil
- tomato paste
- apple cider vinegar (or wine, either white or red is fine)
- 2 cans of whole tomatoes
- dried herbs of choice (I like oregano and thyme)
- crushed chili flakes
- fresh rosemary
- salt
- 4–5 beef short ribs
- Italian flat-leaf parsley (1 bunch)

Steps:

1.) Sear four dry salted short ribs (bone-in) with garlic-infused ghee or oil at a high heat in a Dutch oven or oven-safe large pot.

2.) When all the meat is evenly browned, remove from pot and lower temperature to medium. Add in one to two whole chopped shallots, blocked carrots, double concentrated tomato paste, smashed garlic, and aromatics.

3.) After a few minutes, add apple cider vinegar or wine to deglaze and add beef broth.

4.) Once sufficiently browned, add tomatoes (and optional half a bottle of low sodium marinara sauce). Let simmer to incorporate ingredients before adding back in the short ribs.

5.) After one hour, place covered Dutch oven (if using) in a 325-degree oven until bones easily come out and meat is fork tender. If using a non-oven-safe pot, simmer on low until you reach this texture.

6.) Taste and add pinch of sugar if too acidic, or salt if bland.

7.) Uncover and cook to reduce a little. Cool the sauce before placing it in the refrigerator overnight.

8.) The next day, pull out the top cap of excess fat. It should be solidified and easy to remove. This will lighten up the sauce and not make it too greasy.

9.) Reheat and use sauce for anything! I love this sauce with bread, noodles, and over veggies for a low-carb dinner. Heat up with beef broth if too salty or thick. Enjoy!

When stay-at-home orders began in the US in March 2020, one social media platform, TikTok, achieved huge growth in terms of new users and video content. Tik-Tok became a way to connect with people across the world during an uncertain and anxious time. With the closures of so many restaurant establishments and the unprecedented availability of time, many turned to cooking meals at home. It is not surprising, therefore, that so many creators on the platform rose to fame through the topic of food. Whether it looked like a tutorial on how to replicate Chipotle's guacamole, an explanation of how to cook traditional Italian carbonara, a "What I Eat in a Day" montage, or a video of a mother preparing lunch for her children, "food TikTok" was born. I was able to get in contact with Brittani, who shared her story about how her experiences with two eating disorders have enabled her to help over half a million others who struggle with disordered eating thoughts.

Brittani Lancaster

When I see that I'm helping people recover or gain confidence in themselves, I know that I am making a tangible change. Seeing people be able to love themselves and love who they are because of their unique difference is ultimately most rewarding."

-BRITTANI LANCASTER

Brittani Lancaster is a twenty-two-year-old body positive influencer with a primary platform on TikTok, where she has amassed over eight hundred thousand followers. She became popular on the platform for her "What I Eat in a Day" videos, which feature her meals and snacks over the course of the day as someone in recovery from two eating disorders.

When I interviewed Brittani, I could feel her love of human connection from my computer screen. For her, helping others through their battles with eating disorders is not something she started for TikTok. Rather, she shared her experiences with her friends and sorority members long before she started seriously making videos. After downloading the app in November 2019, she started posting simple videos, mostly meant for her friends and family. In February 2020, however, Brittani posted a video of herself dancing in a dress on her way to her sorority's formal, with the text, "Today marks 3.5 years of eating disorder recovery." The next morning, Brittani woke up to find out her video went viral. At that moment, she realized she could use her platform to inspire positive change in the social media landscape that often reinforces harmful eating behaviors. As a response to the negative implications of the "What I Eat in a Day" video trend, Brittani started documenting her meals in an effort to normalize positive eating behaviors. Previously, this video trend featured tiny portions of meals, unhealthy choices, and ultimately triggered audiences who inadvertently compared their own diets to these unrealistic standards.

As her platform grew, Brittani started receiving positive feedback in her comment sections. As she read countless messages thanking her for her videos and stories of people who had chosen to eat a meal because of her encouragement, she realized her content was truly impacting people and changing lives. Brittani's goal of spreading awareness about disordered eating and destigmatizing shame in the community was realized as she continued to go viral on TikTok.

Like many public figures, however, Brittani began also receiving negative messages as her following grew. Although many commenters in her comment section would immediately defend her against any Internet hater, some took the time to send hateful direct messages. Online hating has negative impacts on not only creators, but also the content they post. When something as triggering as body shaming is sent to a body-positive public figure, it could potentially have negative reverberations to their entire following. Despite this, however, Brittani chose to overcome these voices. When I asked her how she was able to continue unfazed, she said,

"How I've chosen to deal with all of [the hate] is, I always remember that if somebody is willing to go directly to your page and write something so nasty or unkind like that, they are obviously suffering a lot more than you are. They are going through something a lot deeper than you can comprehend. I think most people couldn't even comprehend doing that to somebody they didn't know anything about. You know, I've never left a nasty comment on anybody's post. And I can't even comprehend doing that.

"When I was first experiencing it, it did upset me. Because I feel like that's the normal human reaction to those things. But I've learned to understand that it's not me; rather, it's them, it's something that they're going through."

But the intersection of food and social media did not start on TikTok. TikTok just made its content more interactive and exciting through short videos and its customized algorithm. In actuality, "food TikTok" actually evolved from another social media platform's offering—"food Instagram." Today, more than one out of four Instagram users share food content on the platform, and almost 40 percent of users view food content regularly. One of the most interesting statistics, however, is "foodies" on Instagram connect to the platform four times more than the regular Instagram user. From these observations, it is clear to see food on social media platforms is a highly connective subject matter. Instagram also saw the increase of "food influencers" and hashtags like "#foodporn," "#food," "#foodstagram," and "#foodoftheday."

Whereas food on social media platforms like Instagram and TikTok mainly focused on general communities, more specified communities of food lovers can be created on Facebook groups. One such group, "subtle Asian cooking," focuses on traditional Asian dishes and its users' renditions of it. Although the group consists primarily of those of Asian descent, the group is open for all to join, resulting in the sharing of food, culture, and cooking with a large yet extremely connected community. The group is a subset of the original Facebook "subtle Asian" group, "subtle Asian traits," a group originally consisting of Asian-Australians sharing common experiences for Asians living in primarily English-speaking countries.

YouTube is yet another social media platform with a strong foodie community, but its content contrasts sharply with that of other platforms. Because of the longer-form content typically associated with this platform, "mukbangs," directly translated from Korean to English as "eating room," became its own category of food content. On YouTube, food influencers consume meals (which sometimes consist of exorbitant amounts of fast food) in front of a camera. This content could include the subject consuming food without talking to capture the ASMR aspect of eating, talking about their day or themselves, or telling thrilling stories. The phenomenon of the popularity of "mukbangs" can be directly attributed to the natural human craving for connection, even if it is done virtually. Sitting down in front of a video of another person eating is a comparable experience to eating a meal with a friend, and the comfort of sharing time over food is compelling to so many. Comments from users around the world show how this feeling is mutual for people regardless of their background, proving how the social aspect of food is so universal.

Elliot Norris—Food is Connective Tissue

A huge component of food is its preparation. Cooking is an activity that represents a creative extension of a chef—no matter their skill level.

Elliott Norris is a twenty-five-year-old social media video editor, producer, and content creator based in Los Angeles. For Elliott, food is not only a central part of his French heritage, but it is also a major part of his career as a digital creator on TikTok and Instagram. Initially, cooking was an activity that evoked a sense of relaxation for him. As an influencer who operates in the food world of social media, cooking is a way to unwind and destress from the distractions life presents him. At the same time, however, it is the very way he gathered a following on social media.

Elliott began his social media career with BuzzFeed in 2017, while concurrently working toward his master's degree in marketing through the University of Southern California's School of Cinematic Arts. Elliott pitched a video project idea to the BuzzFeed team and came out with an Instagram TV, or IGTV, series titled *My Gay Kitchen*. On this show, Elliot invited celebrity guests to cook on camera with him in an interactive video format. This longer-form content project in collaboration with BuzzFeed and Instagram propelled Elliot's content to the front of what would be a proliferation of food-related content on Instagram. Today, Elliott posts a condensed version of *My Gay Kitchen* to his more than three hundred thousand TikTok followers on his profile, @callmebelly.

As a sustainability influencer on @getwasted, Elliot aims to share content that brings awareness and recognition to simple sustainable practices that can be adopted fairly easily. Although he makes it a point to share that he himself is not a vegan, plastic-free, or professional, he wants to call attention to how individuals can change aspects of their lifestyles to make them more environmentally friendly.

For instance, though Elliot does enjoy animal protein, like steak and chicken, he will regularly eat plant-based meals on some days of the week, including recipes like washed flour and tofu.

Elliott's platform is primarily based with a specific goal in mind, which is to educate others. Whether he is sharing his healthy recipes, French cooking techniques or dishes, travels across the world, or sustainability practices, Elliot helps his audience broaden its understanding of food. In return, his audience sustains his platform through social media engagement in the form of likes, comments, and shares.

One reason Elliott likes cooking so much is because for him, it is an extremely calming and soothing activity. Before he posts his videos online, he spends time cooking and developing recipes as a form of relaxation and familiarity. In centering himself before producing online content, Elliot uses food as if it were connective tissue— not simply amongst others, but also within himself.

Although food content on different social media plat-forms differs in terms of its audience, purpose, and com-position, food on social media has one common factor: they all exist to connect people to others, whether that be in the form of shared experiences and food cravings or restaurant recommendations.

But the only reality of social media is that it does not reflect reality. Like a lot of content on social media today, a lot of food content shows a different story to what is actually happening behind the scenes. I imagine I was so addicted to these types of videos because I felt as though I was living vicariously through these people, except I wouldn't have to feel guilty about eating. I thought this was harmless at the time, but in reality, I was feeding my disordered mind more lies about food while restricting my body by ignoring hunger cues. I remember feeling the hungriest before going to sleep. Instead of getting a snack from the kitchen, I would watch these videos and feel my stomach growling before I heard it. Like me, many viewers may see an influencer consuming ten thousand calories easily in a day, but they do not get to see the harsh restric-tion that happens the next day, in an influencer's attempt to counteract the effects of overeating for interesting con-tent. I was one such user who was mesmerized by these influencers' abilities to eat such large amounts of food and not face any obvious physical repercussions.

Stephanie Buttermore—Going All-In

Stephanie Buttermore is one such YouTube personal-ity who built a following from food content, specifically her "cheat day" videos. Although her content originally focused on weight training and fitness, her channel saw large growth after her "cheat day eats" videos, which featured her consuming thousands of calories almost effortlessly.

In June of 2019, Stephanie posted an entirely different video, entitled "I Am Going ALL IN | Why Am I So Hungry?" This video exposed the realities of her incredible cheat day videos, her unhappiness, and extreme hunger, which resulted from restriction. In this video, she explained what her "all-in" journey meant. Instead of following a strict diet, she would practice intuitive eating, making sure to eat to satiety until her body regulated her hunger levels and normalized them. For most people, sharing a process that would definitely include weight gain sounds scary. For a female influencer with a large following in the fitness and nutrition space, gaining weight so publicly could not only threaten her career, but also negatively impact her mental headspace. Despite this, Stephanie continued to document her journey, which included highs, like decreased hunger levels, and lows, like mental breakdowns and tears. Although her past content had viewers shocked at what seemed like a superhuman ability to consume food, her new content was focused on the reality of her journey.

One year later, in June 2020, Stephanie posted a video, "How 1 YEAR Of Weight Gain Changed My Life Forever (All In Results!)," that described her process of relearning how to eat and listen to her body, her progress in terms of hunger levels, and the setbacks and lows of her journey.[16] One of the most important topics she discussed was the set point weight theory, which explains each person

16   *Stephanie Buttermore*, "I Am Going ALL IN | Why Am I So Hungry?" uploaded June 5, 2019, Video, 9:58.

has a predetermined weight range that is a result of our genetics. When someone eats too much or too little, the body sends signals to the brain, whether that be in the form of hunger cues or extreme sluggishness.

This was especially clear to me, as I had struggled with fluctuations in my weight when struggling with my own disordered eating patterns in college. Stephanie Buttermore's approach to "all-in" eating revolutionized my inner thoughts about food and led me to reevaluate the content I had been consuming online, even though I am also a creator operating within the food community on Instagram. Without even realizing it, I had been perceiving food-related content online at face value without considering what took place behind the scenes. Underlying the content I consumed was the negative perception that restriction was normal. Even terms like "cheat day" exist because of the assumption that restriction is an everyday thing. Understanding the context in which content is produced is so vital to understanding what "food on social media" really entails. At the same time, it can also lead to a greater appreciation for food content. Behind that recipe video on TikTok are hours of editing, recipe creation, and filming. Behind the YouTube mukbang ASMR video are sound and video editing, practice, and food preparation.

The social media landscape of food is so diverse. It's diverse in terms of content, influencers, and subcategories. Food is a huge part of my own life, so it's not surprising it is also a focal point of my online life. Whether it is through sharing recipes on my cooking Instagram or watching "What I Eat in a Day" videos on TikTok, the landscape of food in social media is extensive. At the same time, as digital citizens, it is now, more than ever, crucial to be a cognizant consumer.

Picturing Food

———

The year 2020 was pivotal for many. The emergence of COVID-19 upended jobs, uprooted people, and ultimately changed what life looked like for everyone. For freshman Miranda Lu, 2020 changed for the better when her first year at university was abruptly cut short by the pandemic.

College, freshman year specifically, can be a difficult transition for many. Some of this difficulty may arise from a loss of support structures, or a nostalgia for the past only exacerbated when facing the uncertainties of the future. For Miranda, freshman year at the University of Southern California would change her outlook on something that used to exist simply as one of the purest sources of her happiness—food.

When thinking about food, most immediately consider what their favorite dishes, tastes, textures, or flavors are. Maybe they even think of their family or friends, a particularly memorable vacation, or their first kitchen. When Miranda thought about food, she thought first about its beauty. While living in Taiwan, before college began for her in the fall of 2019, Miranda would photograph dishes whose remarkable beauty would be enhanced by her meticulous editing skills. She uploaded these photos on VSCO, a photo editing and sharing app, and started to connect with others who shared her love for food photography. From dishes like soft shell crab over squid ink pasta to matcha lattes with intricate espresso art, her account, @matchafoodx, represented her love of the food aesthetic and her celebration of all things beautiful. Her photos, which are dated back to late 2017, are a journey for their viewers, and though they may not be able to translate the taste of these meals, they are truly a feast for the eyes—exactly as she had intended them to be.

Unfortunately, that would turn out to be the problem. Her account was meant to share beauty and creativity with the world; it was a photo journal documenting both fine dining and casual snacks, proving food can be so much more than a meaningless part of one's daily routine. In sharing a part of her life with online audiences at a time when her own insecurities in life started to take root, Miranda became obsessive about her posts. Instead of posting photos as an extension of her creativity, she started posting photos for validation, for others to observe and compliment. Although editing and posting photos of food used to be a creative pastime, it devolved into work. Soon, the simple visual of the editing app filled her with dread as Miranda tried to balance the social pressures of college life, in person and online. As an impressionable freshman in college, Miranda simultaneously lost the close comfort of familial support systems miles away, the closeness of her tight-knit circle of high school friends, and her passion for beautiful foods.

Miranda's relationship with food would become even more complicated than she anticipated. Food became her confidant, but also her enemy. With the stress of freshman year came the dreaded implications of the "freshman fifteen," or the phenomenon, aptly titled, when first-year students at universities gain weight upward of fifteen pounds because of habits like binge drinking and unlimited dining hall options. The more Miranda's mental health deteriorated, the more she began to yield control over food to deal with the stressors that plagued her. She recalls balancing her mental state with the social pressures of fitting in was "exhausting," and her anxieties spanned from academic to social.

One of the main ways to "fit in" or make friends in freshman year at a typical university is to share a meal together in one of the dining halls. Dining halls are not just a one-stop for food, they are also a social space for students to connect with each other. For some, going alone to the dining hall is a daunting task, as the fear of eating in solitude while surrounded by groups of people can be more than overwhelming. Although Miranda engaged in these impromptu gatherings in the same way as most freshmen, the actualities of these events drained Miranda, physically and emotionally. For her, attending one of these spontaneous dinners resulted in eating two dinners and becoming uncomfortably full—a fate that, to her, still felt better than spending the night alone in her dorm room and missing out on experiences that could change the trajectory of her entire college social life. So, it became her cycle. First, she would binge on snacks in her dorm room after class to regain some sense of control over a life that felt so unfamiliar to her. Then, after receiving a text to grab dinner at the dining halls, she would force herself to maintain the guise of a big smile and an empty stomach, because physical discomfort was always tolerable when compared to FOMO, or the fear of missing out.

As she continued to half-heartedly share food on social media platforms, she was often questioned by her friends in the form of a misguided compliment. "How do you eat all of that and still stay so skinny?" "Your metabolism must be so fast!" Despite their positive intentions, these comments only exacerbated Miranda's poor body image and self-worth. What these observers didn't realize was these photos put forth on social media were only part of a larger picture. While it is easy to assume the life of a typical "Instagram model" who shows off their physical assets may look different than their edited or perfectly posed photos, most don't consider the same may apply to any content creator on social media, despite their subject matter. For instance, what people didn't understand about Miranda's relationship with food was that it was devolving into something much darker than the beautifully edited photos on her social media showed. Not only did Miranda struggle with feelings of immense guilt and regret after eating these meals broadcasted on her social media, but she would develop an unhealthy obsession with exercise. She exercised with the purpose of burning the calories she had binged earlier, which she would obsessively document on her smartwatch—as if calories were currency she could deposit and withdraw in her personal bank. Like a shopaholic, however, Miranda was in a constant state of insecurity—but for her, it impacted her mental state, not her finances.

As Miranda struggled to regain control over her eating patterns, she grew more and more weary, and started to lose her love for life—and its inherent beauty.

When COVID-19 sent students across the nation back home, it was actually a relief. Miranda returned home to Taiwan, where her support systems were, and got the help she needed from therapy and maternal support. Today, Miranda is in recovery from her past binge-eating habits. What does "in recovery" mean? From my personal experiences as well as my conversations with those who have struggled with similar habits, being "in recovery" looks different for everyone. To be in the process of recovering from an eating disorder is to unlearn the ingrained behaviors that may feel like muscle memory. It means some days may feel harder than most. It is a battle both with the body and with the mind; realigning your mentality toward food can be a slow, gradual process, and its effects may not be felt until retrospection.

For Miranda, recovery looked like seeking help from her parents in the form of professional therapy. It meant interacting with people who understand and empathize with her struggles, not just as an impressionable freshmen and young adult, but also as a person whose mental struggles had started to impact her physical health. Although "recovery" looks different for everyone, it certainly does not mean it is a perfect solution for all. Eating tendencies and triggers may crop up during someone's life, and that person may fall prey to their past disordered eating habits. But these isolated events only go to prove the fact recovery is many things, but it is not linear. A one-off binge may leave someone feeling guilty and may prompt them to consider old, unhealthy behaviors. The beauty of recovery is that glimpses of one's past lifestyle are just that—glimpses.

Personally, recovery for me is the process of wanting to better your life in whatever means possible. Yes, there will be setbacks, some larger than others, but the worst thing someone can do in these circumstances is let them derail their progress. As someone who has struggled with multiple eating disorders, I can attest to how EDs change your relationship with food permanently. Even as I conquered my fear foods, I struggled to appreciate my progress and truly love who I am.

My Eating Disorder

For as long as I can remember, I have always had a complicated relationship with food.

At a young age, I became obsessed with the ideal of an eerily thin figure, and this unhealthy desire only became exacerbated when I started my formal dance training at seven years old. Although my dance training helped me understand my body better and become stronger, looking at my reflection and hearing my teachers emphasize the importance of a slim, yet muscular physique contributed to my negative feeling of overall discomfort in my own skin. I was small, but hearing such praise for something that seemed out of someone's control felt...wrong.

At this time, I opted to eat tiny portions of food or skip meals entirely. My appetite was small, and my body reflected it as I reveled in the praise from my dance instructors, extended family members, friends, and parents of friends who complimented my "skinniness." I vividly recall driving home with my mom one day while listening to a radio station. As we listened, an advertisement for diet pills started playing, and I joked, "I need that." I think it was at this moment my mom realized the extent of my body dysmorphia, and she angrily drove me home and led me to a computer, where she showed me a

Google image search of "anorexia." This visceral display of human skeletons frightened me at first, but I slowly developed an unhealthy fascination with skinny bodies, and this "ideal" remained ingrained in my mind for years to come. I am lucky my early disordered eating patterns phased out with the help of my family and growing up, yet I recognize how these formative years led to later years of food-controlled behavior.

I stopped dancing my junior year of high school, when I suffered a knee injury that prevented me from continuing the sport. The transition from dancing twenty to thirty hours a week to a more sedentary lifestyle was a big one, and I naturally gained weight and lost muscle as my body adapted to this huge change. As I found myself with more free time to spend with my friends and a new driver's license, I started eating out more, with most of my options being unhealthy, cheap meals. I wasn't consuming McDonald's every day, but I would prioritize hanging out with my friends, which inevitably meant eating out. As I worked part-time jobs, my schedule became even more busy, to the point where virtually all of my lunch and dinner meals were eaten at restaurants or in my car. By the end of my senior year, I weighed thirty-five pounds more than my freshman year initial weight. Granted, some of that weight was just a side effect of puberty and growing older, but this dramatic change was accompanied by losing massive amounts of muscle, strength, and energy. At this point, I didn't feel too much guilt associated with my eating, but I knew my habits weren't the healthiest.

As time passed, I started to become insecure about how I looked to others. Although my weight gain was dramatic, it was gradual to an extent, meaning that although others did not see the change, I felt the impacts of my changing body. I told myself gaining weight was a natural process in this chapter of my life. I masked my unhealthy binges under the pretense of body positivity, and it was only later I realized how skewed my perception of myself was. Fueling your body should never leave you with a loss of control.

Although I was successful at masking this insecurity at first, it was during my freshman year of college and the summer I spent in South Korea prior to the trip I entered into a vicious cycle of self-doubt, hatred, and comparison. Walking around South Korea during the summer is sure to be a hot, humid experience, so I *wore* clothes that reflected the weather. I clearly remember feeling a bit out of place, as I glanced at so many slender figures more covered than I.

For context, although South Korea is home to a massive food culture, it is also a country that praises diets and weight loss to the extreme. From billboards, magazine covers, and ads covering Seoul, its capital city, South Korea's emphasis on unhealthy beauty standards cannot go unnoticed. South Korea is the birthplace of K-pop, a pop-culture wave that spread awareness of Korea, beginning with music, across the globe. K-pop artists are typically extremely skinny and share their diets online, which only perpetuate unhealthy eating standards. These diets range from only eating sweet potatoes, only drinking meals, and even only eating boiled chicken breast and vegetables. Another thing about Korean celebrity culture, especially regarding K-pop "idols," is the relationship between a fan and a celebrity. Idols, for the most part, are expected to partake in "fan-service," or please their fans through meetups, special concerts, videos, or social media engagement. One of the defining factors in an idol-fan relationship that accounts for the phenomenon of "fan-service" is the approachability of an idol. For many fans, these idols aren't some distant celebrities; rather, they are role models and friends.

Therefore, these crazy diets many idols claim are not that far removed from mass culture, and fans and non-fans become exposed to the idea skinny equals beautiful extremely early on. In Korea, body positivity is formed in tandem with underlying assumptions that the normal is the beauty standard. According to "nicer" media channels, to be bigger is to be "brave," to be "overly confident," but what many don't realize is that a backhanded compliment can hurt more than none at all.

As I traveled that summer, I fell prey to this diet culture. I felt huge in comparison, and I purchased some longer, baggier clothes despite the hot weather, and donned sunglasses to shield myself from the gazing, judgmental eyes I perceived to be everywhere—on the subway, in clothing stores, in restaurants, and some even in my temporary residence. No one ever came up to me and said anything, but I felt crippled with insecurity. Not only was I an outsider in terms of my nationality, but I was also an outsider in terms of my physical appearance—or so I thought. After I landed back at LAX in Los Angeles, something in me had changed. I had left the happier, confident Amenda in South Korea, and in her place was the same person with a little more baggage and a little more self-doubt.

My budding insecurity planted its roots a week later, when I moved out of my childhood home to my college dorm room. I lived in a suite with seven other beautiful girls, and my tendency to compare went into overdrive as I contemplated how my lifestyle, fashion, eating habits, and mannerisms fit into theirs. Thankfully, these girls never intentionally tried to trigger these thoughts; rather, it was the overflow of a constantly self-critical mind working overtime.

By the end of my first semester, I had developed the beginnings of what would become a two-year battle with insomnia and anxiety. I recall fighting my mind for the peace that would evolve into sleep. After so many restless nights, I started changing what I ate. I binged a lot my first semester, as many freshmen do, and sometimes my binges would become a false show of confidence and humor. I pretended to be unconcerned with calorie counting and restriction, trademarks of disordered eating, in front of my peers and indulged myself in front of them, acting like I was proud of eating huge amounts of calories, because that made me different—it made me seem as though I was more than the unconfident, small person I had become.

A photo of me freshman year

I began the keto diet in October of 2018, despite familial and friends' concerns about the safety of the diet. I was adamant that as long as I lost even a few pounds, it would all be worth it. I dismissed my friends' worry when I developed a skin condition called "<u>prurigo pigmentosa</u>," commonly known as the "keto rash." For me, the numbers on the scale were more compelling than reason. I was so obsessed with numbers and restriction that I ignored all the signs my poor body was giving me. I became more and more sluggish, was perpetually dizzy, and had low energy, and overindulging myself on high-fat foods ultimately made me sicker and sicker.

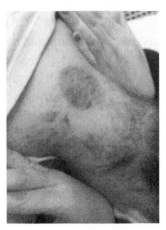

My keto rash in New York. Despite how bad it was, I completely ignored my friends' and family's concern and stubbornly refused to accept that it was a direct result of keto.

During winter break, I gave up keto during a trip to New York with my new university friends and entered into a new cycle of binge eating; this time, the cycle was even stronger because of the forgoing of the high restrictions I had placed on myself for months. One day in Greenwich Village, I sat at a French cafe, waiting for my friend to join me. Instead of waiting for her to arrive, I could not help but eat two entire baguettes before she came. These binges were a result of my complete loss of control when it came to food. Because of the food restriction I had endured for three months, my body was constantly in a state of food-centered thought. My metabolism was weak, my body was discolored, and my anemia had returned, but all I thought about was what I could enjoy for my next meal.

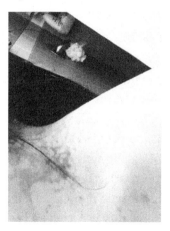

Photos of my keto rash.

Recovering from the keto diet was rough, and seeing such a lack of results disheartened me, as I returned to California only to find I had regained the few pounds I had lost. After scouring the Internet and ending up in a black hole characterized by MyPlate, MyFitnessPal, and Reddit communities like r/1200isplenty, I came to yet another misguided conclusion. The only way I could scientifically lose weight was through calorie deficit. The issue was that at the time, the words "restriction" and "deficit" were synonymous. I began eating small portions, meticulously calculating each meal on MyFitnessPal. Soon, 1,600 calories seemed like enough, and then 1,400, and eventually, 1,200 did become plenty in my twisted mind. I remember laying wide awake in my twin XL bed at 3:00 a.m., not being able to sleep and feeling the gnawing hunger in my empty stomach. I would reassure myself this was a good problem to have and a sign it would all be worth it in the end.

What I didn't realize at the time was how this diet was just another type of restriction that would ultimately leave my body hungering for more. My skewed view of the world and how I fit into it was fueled in part by one of my hometown best friends who was going through a similar thing. Although our relationship with each other in the context of eating was toxic, there was an eerie sense of comfort in restricting and purging together—as if becoming skinnier would make us happy and solve all our problems. The reality was this cycle exacerbated our sadness and created more problems as we cast a critical eye onto our every action.

The summer after sophomore year, I visited South Korea again, but this time, I stayed with my great-aunt and great-uncle in Seoul, South Korea. With their help, my great-aunt in particular, I started to really see myself through the eyes of others. Every day, she would give me a positive affirmation about my looks or character. By no means was I a representation of the Korean beauty standard, with my tanned skin, darker makeup, and sometimes less than modest clothing. However, the affirmations she told me and the delicious food she cooked me helped me start to regain my confidence and, therefore, begin the difficult journey of recovery and self-love. As school started that fall and I moved to my first apartment, I tried to think less about food, but fell victim to my last eating disorder: orthorexia nervosa.

Orthorexia nervosa, or orthorexia, is an eating disorder that often goes undiagnosed. Those with orthorexia have a strong fixation on "healthy eating" or nutrition to the point where it starts to negatively impact the person in question's physical, mental, and emotional state of mind.[17] For me, my orthorexia was marked with a feeling of power in cooking only healthy meals and meal prepping for the week. Those close to me would praise my healthy habits, often saying things like "You're so healthy!" or "I wish I could eat as healthy as you." I reveled in this praise, and even started a food Instagram, @mendameals, full of my recipes I marketed as "cheap, healthy recipes for the broke college student." In my first post, I documented my breakfast: a cup of coffee with cashew milk and a small yogurt bowl. Similar posts would follow, like an egg white spinach scramble with celery lemon juice.

---

17   "Orthorexia," Internet & Technology, National Eating Disorder Association, 2018.

Screenshots of some of these typical Instagram posts that exemplified my negative, calculating behaviors regarding food.

Instead of consuming food, food was consuming me, my thoughts, and my actions.

The worst part of this was I was inadvertently triggering some of the people I lived with—my roommates and close friends. I projected my fear of unhealthy foods onto them, and although I indulged in unhealthy meals and snacks with them, I would constantly speak about calories, or how unhealthy a food would be. One example of my extreme attention to food was my need for control over our communal meals. I needed to be the one cooking, not just because I loved to cook at the time, but because I needed to know what was going into my meals. I didn't want beef meatballs with a high percentage of fat—I preferred turkey. I used spaghetti squash in lieu of the actual pasta I was really craving. I wiped cooking pans with a paper towel after pouring oil in them so only the most minimal amount of oil would be in my food. I thought I was being healthy, but I was making food so much more complicated than it needed to be. Thankfully, I was able to have this realization before my mind-set progressed. Unfortunately, this mind-set is all too common, as we consume harmful media that reinforces bad eating behavior from public figures claiming to be "nutrition and fitness influencers."

In growing obsessed with recipe development, "healthy" substitutes, and meal preparation, I lost sight of the initial reason I grew concerned about food—I just wanted to be healthy and happy. As I started to shift my mentality to one of true health rather than calculated health, I began to see improvements not only in my mental state, but also my physical one. I remember in the depths of my eating disorders that occurred in college, I would examine myself in my full body mirror in the morning, and my perception of myself would set the tone for the day. For example, if I had eaten a large dinner or binged the night before, seeing my reflection in the mirror was frustrating, and I would carry that anger with me for the rest of the day. Inversely, if I woke up to a de-puffed face and flat stomach, I would start the day cheerfully, happy I had the body (at least for the day) I so wanted. During this time, I also experienced one of the worst depressive episodes of my life, and I can clearly tie my ED to this instance. The issue was my happiness was so dependent on superficial things. When my emotions were tied to things like weight, or my reflection, I was in a constant cycle of self-critique, self-hatred, but also self-love. This made it extremely difficult to recognize I even had a problem—happiness is not sustainable unless it comes from a true acceptance of the self.

Recovery is not easy. Recovery for me meant I had to let go of a lot of "security blankets" I had wrapped myself up in. To this day, I can probably tell you within how many calories are approximately in a common food item. To this day, I may sometimes feel weird after eating out with friends. To this day, I struggle with loving my body all the time. Recovery is definitely not linear, and what I consider as part of my recovery may seem abnormal to some.

As the author of this book, I want to be as transparent as possible with my readers. As much as I love food and have a passion for cooking, food is not something I have always had an easy relationship with. If you relate with any of the struggles I mentioned in this chapter, I would love to offer some tools and actions I took that were especially helpful in my recovery.

- The best advice I could give anyone struggling with self-love and insecurities surrounding their body is to think about what their older self would be saying to them. Ten years down the road, I don't want to look back and wonder why I was so insecure, hard on myself, or limited by my own negativity. I want to appreciate this time, this golden time when opportunities are ripe, and everything contributes to personal growth—especially my failures.

- Be cognizant about the fact the world speaks to individuals in generalizations. You've probably heard some of them that relate to the human body. The problem is these generalizations do not necessarily hold true for every individual. Develop an awareness of what you are consuming on social media, and the influencers you follow. Following a fitness influencer on Instagram two years ago would have been extremely toxic for me, but now, as I learn to listen to my body's needs, I realize how necessary exercise is for my physical and mental health. Therefore, I engage with fitness content regularly on social media, learning from some influencers but also taking advice with a grain of salt—because we are individuals with unique needs and bodies.

- Engage in self-reflection. I found that a huge hinderance for me was my constant need to be doing something. I was always multitasking, even when I was doing something I loved, liked cooking. Where did that constant need to be overstimulated come from? Definitely part of it can be attributed to our generation's unprecedented engagement with technology and media, but it was also partly just my personality. When I stopped doing a thousand things at once, I learned to spend time with myself and my thoughts. Not all of these thoughts were positive at first, but as I spent more and more time alone with myself, I learned how self-reflection could help me understand myself, my motivations, and my goals in life. When I set my identity not in my outward appearance, but my internal one, I was able to learn a confidence that could not be shaken with menial things like my reflection in a mirror.

- Don't try to immediately make drastic changes to your life—they're unsustainable, as you probably know. When I weighed the most, I decided to commit myself to the gym for three hours a day. After three days, I decided to skip the fourth day, and then didn't return to the gym until the next school year. Because I was working out to achieve a goal of losing the weight I had gained, rather than to be strong or healthy, I was unable to commit to exercising regularly. Worse than that, I developed an unhealthy relationship with fitness and working out. Going to the gym was a punishment for my binges, a retribution for losing control yet again to food. But who in their right mind would ever willingly engage in regular punishment? Thus, when my motivation for working out stemmed from anything food-related, it did not last. Before I could physically train my body to exercise and really enjoy it, I had to be at peace with my inner self. Train your mind first before your try to train your body.

- Intuitive eating sounds simple, but it can actually be difficult for many in recovery. For me, starting to intuitively eat was hard because I had forgotten what my hunger cues were. I only knew of two feelings: dire hunger or extreme fullness. To intuitively eat, I had to relearn my hunger cues and change my habits slowly. Instead of waking up in the morning and following the same routine, I decided to shake it up. Instead of a black coffee and protein bar, I would make an omelet. I started to disassociate cooking with calories, and instead associated it with creativity and experimentation. Sooner than I anticipated, I started to listen to my body and realize when what I was feeling was moderate hunger or perfect fullness.

Finally, remember all art romanticizes life. Life itself can be less-than-perfect most of the time, and art offers a reprieve from some scary realities. Start to romanticize your own life. Remember, food is the currency of love. Love is romanticized by art. Art is food. And most importantly, you are the art in the context of your life.

Conclusion

———

Food has always been a central part of my life. Whether my relationship with it manifested itself in positive or negative ways, food has been a constant; more than an interest, but an extension of the self. For me, writing this book allowed me to really understand the sociology and underlying systems that shape our relationships around food. Although my initial plan was to share my discoveries and personal experiences about human connections through this book, I found these relationships are far more complex and deep-rooted than I initially thought.

In Part One, I spoke on some of the connections that actually inspired this book. After writing this section, I felt like something important was missing. In my life and in my writing, I aim to be my most genuine, authentic self. As reflected in my writing, I decided to narrate my own journey and relationship with food as I remember it. In writing this, I realized I had only focused on the parts of my life that I found joy in food and love in cooking. But these positive interactions with food didn't tell the whole story. To make this book unapologetically me, and in turn, help others, I decided to write about my struggles with the debilitating eating disorders that shaped my life and my sense of self-worth. These painful memories reminded me that for all the love I had for food, I also had times in my life where I hated food, and my writing a book about only my positive experiences would be a perpetuation of my insecurities.

As I embraced this shift in subject matter, I found that disordered eating patterns is a common issue many are actually willing to speak up about. I also educated myself about the food systems in place in our world that hinders the world's ability to appreciate and express themselves through food. Thus, Part Two of my book was born. Although the subjects I speak on in this chapter are heavier, I hope it resonates with you, the reader, and helps you broaden your understanding of why food is complicated. In the same way writing this book took me on a journey unearthing these relationships and connecting them to my life, I hope you have had a similar experience reading it.

Because eating is something that is very routine for many of us, we often take it for granted. But for humans, food serves a twofold purpose. Many people, including me, sometimes only focus on one of those purposes, which is that food is a unit of energy and a physical nourisher. But food is also something that is connective, a facilitator of spiritual, mental, and emotional nourishment. It is only when we recognize *both* these definitions of food that we can delve into the complex and poignant relationships that can come out of our relationships with food, cooking, or eating.

Food is easy to define, but the implications that come from it are more difficult to pin down. Exploring the intersections between food and art, cultures, faith, creativity, justice, personal growth, and relationships only proves how food can be a medium for social and interpersonal connections. While food is an incredible subject matter in improving our understanding of our world, it is also a hindrance for some who struggle with disorderly eating patterns.

The recipes I included throughout this book represent parts of me that I cherish. They are memories of people, places, and experiences that have made a significant experience in my life. I hope these recipes help you understand my stories, and those of others, better. If you do make any of my recipes, please tag me @mendameals on Instagram. I would love to see your iteration of my creations!

Whoever you are, I hope reading this book has helped you reflect upon your own experiences with food that have shaped your life and the relationships you have forged because or in spite of it. I truly believe one's relationships with food is not something that is fixed. My own journey recovering from the disordered eating patterns that defined my life and consumed my thoughts is proof of that, as is my continual growth in terms of cooking techniques and practices in the kitchen. When we value food, we become more in tune with ourselves and how we fit into this world.

Acknowledgments

Writing this book was not simply months of self-reflection. The publication of this book would have not been possible without the guidance, help, and input from the following people:

My Family:

James Lee, my dad, who has always impressed upon me the value of hard work and cultural connection.

Janet Lee, my mom, who taught me how to cook and fostered my love of food and for people.

Samantha Lee, my older sister, who has humbled me and facilitated my growth as a person and friend.

Halmoni and Halabogi, my grandparents, whose lives inspire me to live my own to the fullest.

My Friends:

Anaïs Connelly, my best friend, who has encouraged me, fueled my passion for food, and been a confidant, a muse, and my biggest cheerleader.

Tiffany Kim, my best friend of seventeen years, who has been with me through absolutely everything and continues to do so.

James, Andrew, Brandon, Elliot, and Kevin, my friends, who support my every endeavor and comfort me during my lows.

To everyone who supported this writing process from beginning to end.

Megan Hennessy, my Developmental Editor

Morgan Rhode, my Marketing and Revisions Editor

Professor Eric Koester of the Georgetown University Creator Institute

Beri Harris, who has encouraged my writing dreams since high school

To those who supported my first writing endeavor and the early presales of my book.

Audrea Huang	Sam Budiartho
Sam Lee	Eunice Kim
Tony Kam	Joanna Lee
Anaïs Connelly	Tiffany Kim
Min Ju Kang	Miranda Lu
James Lai	Claire Kim
Janet Lee	Hannah Choi
Jacquelyn Aramkul	Jun Cho
James Lee	Sarah Lee
Joon Won Lee	George Parampathu
Tommy Chang	Eric Koester
Keun Umma	Andrew Hess

Lois Lee
Sarah Kang
Joshua Hung
Jean Mok
Jackie Yim
William Huang
Andrew Kim
Sophie Tan
Susan Yoon
Jacob Soll
Annie Kim
Tony Kim
Achinta McDaniel
Samantha Mickelson
Audrey Burba
Christina Kim
Joanne Seung
June Hess
Shirley Nguyen
Anjali Chary
Ankita Pattnaik
Jamie Cho

Stella Hess
Florence Liu
Beri Harris
Mady Kim
Kelly Peterson
Brandon Hulston
Kecy Sun
Linda Guite
Juwon Lee
Elliot Myong
Karina Sun
Wenny Chou
Hendel Benito Charles
Claire Choe
Ellecia Williams
Esther Cha
Najwa Bou-Melhem
Jane Hwang
Hala Khalifeh
James Lai
Ryan Lee

Appendix

———

Breaking Bread and Baking Bread

Alinea Restaurant Group. "Awards for Alinea." Accessed January 1, 2021. https://www.thealineagroup.com/awards/Alinea.

Boal, Augusto. Theater of the Oppressed. New York: Theater Communications Group, 1985.

Gross, Terry, and Grant Achatz. *Grant Achatz: The Chef Who Couldn't Taste*. Produced by NPR. Interview, MP3 Audio. https://www.npr.org/transcripts/139786504.

Max, D. T. "A Man of Taste: A chef with cancer fights to save his tongue." *New Yorker, May 12, 2008. https://www.newyorker.com/magazine/2008/05/12/a-man-of-taste.*

National Eating Disorder Association. "Orthorexia." Internet and Technology. 2018. https://www.nationaleatingdisorders.org/learn/by-eating-disorder/other/orthorexia.

The Three Fs: Food, Friends, Family

Bramen, Lisa. "Good Night and Good Potluck." *Smithsonian Magazine,* May 25, 2010. https://www.smithsonianmag.com/arts-culture/good-night-and-good-potluck-89186862/.

Wells, Chris. *"The Potluck, A Native American Thanksgiving Tradition?"* The Houston Museum of Natural Science: Beyond Bones. November 16, 2016. https://blog.hmns.org/2016/11/the-potluck-a-native-american-thanksgiving-tradition/.

Eating through the City: Los Angeles

U.S. Department of Commerce, Bureau of the Census. *QuickFacts: Los Angeles County, California, 2020.* Ann Arbor, MI, 2020. https://www.census.gov/quickfacts/losangelescountycalifornia.

Food Equality and Justice

FoodPrint. "Food Justice." FoodPrint. Accessed November 13, 2020. https://foodprint.org/issues/food-justice/.

The Time to Throw Out the Melting Pot

History. "U.S. Immigration Timeline." Internet & Research. Updated September 3, 2019. https://www.history.com/topics/immigration/immigration-united-states-timeline.

Library of Congress. "Immigration and Relocation in U.S. History." Internet & Research. Updated 2021. https://libwww.freelibrary.org/programs/onebook/.

San Diego Government. "Timeline of Immigration to the United States." Internet & Research. Updated January 2021.

https://www.sandiego.gov/sites/default/files/timeline_
of_immigration_to_the_us.pdf.

Social Media and Food

Stephanie Buttermore. "I Am Going ALL IN | Why Am I So Hungry?" Uploaded June 5, 2019. Video, 9:58. https://www.
youtube.com/watch?v=DotlyWhBhak&ab_channel=StephanieButtermore.

My Eating Disorder

National Eating Disorder Association. "Orthorexia." Internet
and Technology. 2018. https://www.nationaleatingdisorders.org/learn/by-eating-disorder/other/orthorexia.